2

Second Edition

NETWORK+
CERTIFICATION

ACADEMIC LEARNING SERIES

LAB MANUAL

PUBLISHED BY
Microsoft Press
A Division of Microsoft Corporation
One Microsoft Way
Redmond, Washington 98052-6399

Library of Congress Cataloging-in-Publication Data
Network+ Certification Training Kit.--2nd ed.
      p. cm.
    Includes index.
    ISBN 0-7356-1456-3
    ISBN 0-7356-1770-8 (Academic Learning Series)
    1. Computer networks--Examinations-Study guides. I. Microsoft Corporation.

TK5105.5 .N4652   2001
004.6'076--dc21   2001044545

Printed and bound in the United States of America.

1 2 3 4 5 6 7 8 9   QWT   7 6 5 4 3 2

Distributed in Canada by H.B. Fenn and Company Ltd.

A CIP catalogue record for this book is available from the British Library.

Microsoft Press books are available through booksellers and distributors worldwide. For further information about international editions, contact your local Microsoft Corporation office or contact Microsoft Press International directly at fax (425) 936-7329. Visit our Web site at www.microsoft.com/mspress. Send comments to *tkinput@microsoft.com*.

For Microsoft Press
Acquisitions Editor: Kathy Harding
Project Editor: Julie Miller

Author: Craig Zacker

SubAsy Part No. X08-92413
Body Part No. X08-92415

For IQUAD Solutions
Project Manager: Ila Neeley
Copy Editor: Merianne Marble
Technical Editor: Rich Hillyard
Desktop Publisher: Cathy Gilmore

Introduction

This Lab Manual supplements the *ALS: Network+ Certification, Second Edition* textbook. The labs in this manual are designed to be performed in a classroom environment by a group of students under the supervision of an instructor.

The labs in this manual are intended to reinforce and build upon the concepts presented in the textbook and are an essential part of your training. The opportunity to explore both the hardware and software aspects of network administration in this Lab Manual will provide the valuable experience and skills that are required of the entry-level networking professional, as well as a valuable preparation tool for the Network+ certification exam.

The labs in this manual are performed in a classroom that is configured as an isolated internetwork. Initially, the computers in the classroom are configured as Microsoft Windows 2000 workgroups, where each student (or group of students) has two computers that comprise an independent workgroup network, with a name assigned by the instructor. As you work your way through the labs, you will modify the configuration of your workgroup network and connect it to the classroom network as needed.

Network+ certification is a testing program sponsored by the Computing Technology Industry Association (CompTIA) that certifies the competency of network technicians in the computer industry. Earning Network+ certification means that you possess the knowledge, skills, and customer-relations expertise that are essential for a successful networking professional. If you are seeking Network+ certification, the labs in this Lab Manual will form an important part of your preparation.

Contents

Lab 1: Networking Basics

Objectives

After completing this lab, you will be able to

- Install Network Monitor on a computer running Microsoft Windows 2000 Server
- Configure Network Monitor
- Capture and view network traffic
- Understand the data encapsulation process by viewing the protocols at the various layers of the Open Systems Interconnection (OSI) reference model
- Customize a display filter

Note Completing this lab will help reinforce your learning from Chapter 1 of the textbook.

Before You Begin

To complete this lab, you will need the following information:

- The password for the Administrator account on your workgroup server, assigned by your instructor.
- The two-digit number assigned to your workgroup by your instructor. This number is used to form the name of your workgroup (WG*xx*, where *xx* is the number assigned to your workgroup) and the name of your workgroup server (WG*xx*Svr).
- A user name and password providing you with access to the Instructor01 server on the classroom network.

Estimated time to complete the lab: 30 minutes

Exercise 1
Installing Network Monitor

In this exercise, you will install Network Monitor so you can capture and analyze network traffic throughout this course.

▶ **To install Network Monitor**

1. Log on to the workgroup server as Administrator, using the password supplied by your instructor.

2. Click Start, point to Programs, point to Accessories, and then click Command Prompt.

   The Command Prompt window appears.

3. In the Command Prompt window, type **ipconfig /all** and then press ENTER.

   What IP address is your computer using?

   10. 41. 213. 17

   Where did this address come from?

   DHCP Server - Default Hard copy Server

   In the space below, write the Physical Address value located in the Ethernet Adapter Local Area Connection section of the Ipconfig display.

   00 - 04 - 75 - A9 - A3 - C7

   What does this value represent?

   Hex number and it represents a mac Address, It cannot be changed.

4. Type **exit** in the Command Prompt window, and then press ENTER.

   The Command Prompt window closes.

5. Click Start, point to Settings, and then click Control Panel.

   The Control Panel window opens.

6. Double-click the Add/Remove Programs icon.

   The Add/Remove Programs dialog box appears.

7. Click Add/Remove Windows Components.

   The Windows Components Wizard is launched.

8. On the Windows Components page, scroll down the Components list and select Management And Monitoring Tools, and then click Details.

   The Management And Monitoring Tools dialog box appears.

9. Select the Network Monitor Tools check box, and then click OK to close the dialog box.

10. Click Next.

    The Configuring Components page appears as the wizard begins to copy the appropriate files. After a short delay, an Insert Disk message box appears, instructing you to insert the Windows 2000 Server CD-ROM into the drive.

Note You do not need to insert the CD-ROM. The files you need were installed in the C:\Windist folder on your computer before you began this lab.

---

11. Click OK to display the Files Needed dialog box.

12. Type **c:\windist** in the Copy Files From text box, and then click OK.

    The wizard continues copying files.

Note In some cases, you might be prompted to insert the Windows 2000 Server CD-ROM more than once, but you should ignore those messages, too.

---

13. On the Completing The Windows Components Wizard page, click Finish to close the wizard and complete the installation.

14. Click Close to close the Add/Remove Programs dialog box.

15. Close Control Panel.

Exercise 2
Configuring Network Monitor

In this exercise, you will run Network Monitor for the first time and configure its settings.

▶ **To configure Network Monitor**

1. Click Start, point to Programs, point to Administrative Tools, and then click Network Monitor.

   The Network Monitor – Select Default Network message box appears.

2. Click OK to close the message box.

   The Select A Network dialog box appears.

3. Expand the Local Computer heading and select the network interface adapter containing the Physical Address value you wrote down in Exercise 1, and then click OK.

   The Capture Window appears. The title bar contains the system name of the network interface adapter you just selected, including its physical address.

Note The physical address of the network interface adapter is in hexadecimal form. The Ipconfig display places dashes between the bytes of the address, but the Select A Network dialog box does not.

---

4. On the Capture menu, select Buffer Settings.

   The Capture Buffer Settings dialog box appears.

5. Change the Buffer Size (MB) setting from 1 (its default value) to 10, and then click OK.

Note The capture buffer is an area of the hard disk where Network Monitor temporarily saves the packets it captures from the network. By default, the capture buffer is only 1 MB, but you have just increased it to 10 MB, enabling you to capture more packets at one time. You can increase this value as needed, as long as you have sufficient disk space on the drive.

---

6. On the Capture menu, select Addresses.

   The Address Database dialog box appears.

Note The address database contains the addresses read from captured packets and their equivalent names, when available. Whenever possible, Network Monitor displays packet information using names instead of addresses, which makes it easier for the user to interpret the information.

What is the function of the address database entries that begin with an asterisk (*)?

_____

_____

Which data-link layer protocols does Network Monitor support? How can you tell?

_____

_____

_____

Write down the Name, Address, and Type values for the entries without asterisks.

_____

_____

_____

What do these entries represent?

_____

_____

7. Click the Local entry with the network adapter's physical address (it is often the last entry in the list), and then click Edit.

   The Address Information dialog box appears.

8. In the Name text box, replace LOCAL with the name of the computer (WG*xx*Svr, where *xx* is the number assigned to the workgroup by the instructor).

9. Select the Permanent Name check box, and then click OK.

   How has the entry changed?

_____

_____

10. Click Save.

    The Save Addresses As dialog box appears.

11. Type your last name in the File Name text box, and then click Save.

    The address database entries you modified are saved as the file name you specified, with an .adr extension, located in the C:\WINNT\System32\Netmon folder.

12. Click Close to close the Address Database dialog box.

13. In the Capture Window, on the Capture menu, select Save Configuration.

14. On the File menu, select Exit.

    Network Monitor closes.

Exercise 3
Capturing Network Traffic

In this exercise, you will use Network Monitor to capture and examine network traffic.

▶ **To capture network traffic**

1. Click Start, point to Programs, point to Administrative Tools, and then click Network Monitor.

   The Network Monitor application opens, displaying the Capture Window you saw in Exercise 2.

2. On the Capture menu, select Addresses.

   The Address Database dialog box appears.

3. Click Load.

   The Open Address File dialog box appears.

4. Select the address file you created with your last name in Exercise 2, and then click Open.

5. Click Close to close the Address Database dialog box.

Note Remember to open your address file each time you launch Network Monitor. This action retains the addressing information you have gathered.

---

6. On the Capture menu, select Start.

Tip To start the capture, you can also click the Start Capture icon on the toolbar or press F10.

---

7. Click Start, point to Programs, point to Accessories, and then click Windows Explorer.

8. Browse to the classroom Windows 2000 server (Instructor01) by expanding My Network Places, Entire Network, Microsoft Windows Network, and the Contoso.msft domain.

   The Enter Network Password dialog box appears.

9. Type the domain user name and password provided by your instructor in the Connect As and Password text boxes, and then click OK.

10. Expand the Instructor01 icon and select the Temp share, and then copy the Setuplog.txt file from the Temp share on Instructor01 to the \Temp folder on drive C of your server.

11. Return to Network Monitor, and on the Capture menu, select Stop And View. A new window named Capture: 1 (Summary) opens.

Tip To stop the capture and view the results, you can also click the Stop And View Capture icon on the toolbar or press SHIFT+F11.

12. On the Window menu, select the Capture Window entry (with your network adapter's physical address) to return to the original display.

Study the information shown in the Capture Window, and then answer the following questions.

How many frames were captured to the buffer?

_____

How do you know?

_____

_____

How much space is left in the capture buffer?

_____

How do you know?

_____

_____

What is the physical address of the classroom server?

_____

How do you know?

_____

_____

_____

_____

13. Right-click the physical address in the Network Address 2 column representing the classroom server, and then select the Edit Address *xxxxxxxxxxx* item from the context menu (where *xxxxxxxxxxx* is the physical address).

    The Address Information dialog box appears.

14. Type **Instructor01** in the Name text box, select the Permanent Name check box, and then click OK.

    What happens?

    _____

    _____

    _____

    Why?

    _____

    _____

    _____

    How many bytes have been sent to the Instructor01 server? How can you tell?

    _____

    _____

    _____

Note The version of Network Monitor included with Windows 2000 Server is limited to capturing traffic transmitted to or from the computer it is installed on. As a result, the traffic between the other student servers and Instructor01 does not appear in your Network Monitor statistics, nor can your version of Network Monitor capture those packets. To capture all of the packets on the network, regardless of their source, you must use the version of Network Monitor included with Microsoft Systems Management Server (SMS) 2.0.

---

15. On the Window menu, select Capture: 1 (Summary).

    The Capture: 1 (Summary) window appears.

16. Scroll down in the Capture: 1 (Summary) window and select the first frame that contains Instructor01 in the Src MAC Addr column, your server's name in the Dst MAC Addr column, and NBT in the Protocol column.

The Description column should begin with SS: Session Message. This frame contains part of the Setuplog.txt file you copied from Instructor01 while Network Monitor was capturing packets.

17. Double-click the frame you selected.

The window splits into three segments. The top segment is the summary pane, which contains the frame listing you were just viewing; the middle segment is the detail pane, which contains the interpreted contents of the frame; and the bottom segment is the hex pane, which contains the raw contents of the frame.

18. Adjust the borders between the panes to enlarge the detail pane.

19. Double-click the plus sign (+) next to the Frame: Base Frame Properties entry in the detail pane.

The Frame: Base Frame Properties entry is expanded.

How large is the frame you selected?

_____

Note The length of the frame you selected represents the maximum size for a standard Ethernet packet, including the headers and footer. Frames can be smaller (when they carry less data), but when a file is transmitted that is larger than the maximum Ethernet frame size, the file is broken down in segments small enough to fit into individual frames. In that case, each frame carries 1,460 bytes of actual data (which you can see in the Description column in the summary pane).

20. Expand the ETHERNET entry in the detail pane.

Network Monitor displays the contents of the Ethernet header fields.

Note As you move down in the detail pane entries, you move farther up in the OSI reference model. Each of the protocols operating at the data-link, network, transport, and application layers is represented by an entry in this pane.

At what layer of the OSI model are these header fields located?

_____

What other protocols appear in the detail pane, and at what layers of the OSI model do they operate?

_____

_____

_____

Note You will learn more about the functions of the individual protocol header fields later in this course.

21. On the File menu, select Save As.

    The Save As dialog box appears.

22. Type **Lab1** in the File Name text box, and then click Save.

    Network Monitor copies the contents of the capture buffer to the Lab1.cap file in the C:\WINNT\System32\Netmon\CAPTURES folder.

23. On the File menu, select Exit.

    The Save Address Database? message box appears, reminding you to save the new entries in your address file.

24. Click Yes.

    The Save Addresses As dialog box appears.

25. Select the address file you created earlier, and then click Save.

    Network Monitor closes.

Exercise 4
Using Display Filters

In this exercise, you will use a display filter to control the information that Network Monitor displays. In many cases, Network Monitor captures many different types of packets, and display filters are a means of zeroing in on exactly the frames you want to study.

▶   **To customize a display filter**

1. Click Start, point to Programs, point to Administrative Tools, and then click Network Monitor.

   The Network Monitor application opens, displaying the Capture Window you saw in Exercise 3.

2. On the Capture menu, select Addresses.

   The Address Database dialog box appears.

3. Click Load.

   The Open Address File dialog box appears.

4. Select the address file you created in Exercise 2, and then click Open.

5. Click Close to close the Address Database dialog box.

6. On the File menu, select Open.

   The Open dialog box appears.

7. Select the Lab1.cap file you created in Exercise 3, and then click Open.

   The Summary window for the Lab1.cap file appears.

8. On the Display menu, select Filter.

   The Display Filter dialog box appears.

9. Select the Protocol == Any entry, and then click Edit Expression.

   The Expression dialog box appears.

10. Click Disable All.

    All of the protocols listed in the Enabled Protocols list are moved to the Disabled Protocols list.

11. Scroll down the Disabled Protocols list and select NBT from the Name column, and then click Enable.

    The NBT protocol is moved to the Enabled Protocols list.

12. Click OK.

13. Select the ANY <--> ANY entry, and then click Edit Expression.

    The Expression dialog box appears.

14. In the Station 1 list, select the entry with Instructor01 in the Name column and the classroom server's physical address in the Address column.

15. In the Direction box, select the arrow pointing to the right.

16. In the Station 2 list, select the entry with your computer's name (WG*xx*Svr, where *xx* is the number assigned to your workgroup by the instructor) in the Name column and your computer's physical address in the Address column.

17. In the Expression dialog box, click OK.

18. In the Display Filter dialog box, click OK.

What happens?

_____

_____

_____

Why do other frames, such as those with SMB in the Protocol column, still appear if the display filter is configured to show only NBT frames?

_____

_____

_____

Note Network Monitor also supports capture filters, which you configure by selecting Filter from the Capture menu. Capture filters limit the frames that are saved to the capture buffer, enabling you to capture specific types of traffic for longer periods of time without filling the buffer.

19. On the File menu, select Exit.

Network Monitor closes.

20. Log off the workgroup server.

Lab 2: Networking Hardware

Objectives

After completing this lab, you will be able to

- Recognize the components used to build a small local area network (LAN)
- Install a network interface adapter into a computer
- Assemble the components of a simple LAN
- Configure a network adapter driver

Note Completing this lab will help reinforce your learning from Chapter 2 of the textbook.

Before You Begin

Your instructor should provide you with the following equipment:

- One Ethernet hub with power supply
- One network interface adapter (referred to as a network interface card, or NIC, in this lab)
- Two unshielded twisted-pair (UTP) network cables
- Tools for working on the computer (if needed)
- Static control equipment (antistatic wrist straps or mats)

You will also need the password for the Administrator account on your workgroup workstation, assigned by your instructor.

In this lab, you are supplied with all of the hardware you need to connect the two computers in your workgroup to form a LAN. Your workgroup server is already equipped with a NIC and has been configured to access the classroom network. This configuration allowed you to perform the exercises in Lab 1. Your workgroup workstation, however, does not have a NIC installed. You will install the NIC you have been given into the workstation computer and connect it to your workgroup network.

In this lab, you will build an independent workgroup LAN out of your two computers, so before you begin, be sure to disconnect the workgroup server from the classroom network by unplugging the cable from its NIC.

Estimated time to complete the lab: 30 minutes

Exercise 1
Examining Your Equipment

In this exercise, you are introduced to the hardware components you will use to construct your workgroup network.

▶ **To examine the hub**

Note Hubs differ in design and features. The hub you have been given might not correspond exactly with the instructions given in this section.

1. Remove the hub from its box and examine it on all sides.

   Answer the following questions:

   How many ports does the hub have?

   _____

   How many light-emitting diode (LED) indicators does the hub have?

   _____

   What is the function of the LED indicator associated with each port?

   _____

   _____

   _____

Note The documentation for a hub could be found in a booklet, disk, or CD-ROM. You may also have to consult the manufacturer's Web site for more information about your hub.

2. Locate the uplink port on the hub and answer the following questions:

   What is the function of the uplink port?

   _____

   _____

   Is there a switch associated with the uplink port?

   _____

If so, what is the function of the switch?

_____

_____

_____

▶   **To examine the NIC**

1. Set up the antistatic equipment. This may involve connecting an antistatic mat to a ground and/or putting on a wrist strap and grounding it as well.

2. Open the box containing the NIC, remove it from its packaging, and examine it.

Caution Handle the NIC (and all circuit boards) carefully at all times, trying not to touch the connectors or the components mounted on the board. Do not put the NIC down on an unprotected surface; use an antistatic mat or the antistatic bag the NIC came in.

Answer the following questions:

How many connectors does the NIC have on its slot end, and what type are they?

_____

_____

How many LEDs are on the slot end, and what are their functions?

_____

_____

_____

What type of bus connector does the NIC have?

_____

Are there any jumpers or dual inline package (DIP) switches on the circuit board itself? If so, what are their functions?

_____

_____

3. Put the NIC back into its antistatic bag for protection.

Exercise 2
Installing a NIC

In this exercise, you will install the NIC into the workgroup workstation computer.

▶ **To install a NIC**

1. Shut down the workstation computer (if it is running), and unplug the power cable from the back of the case.

2. Prepare your work area by setting up the antistatic equipment you have been provided.

Caution Always perform these first two safety steps before working inside any computer.

3. Remove the cover from the case and set it aside.

Tip Most computers use thumbscrews, plastic latches, or both to hold the case onto the computer. On older machines, you may have to remove a number of Phillips-head screws to open the case.

4. Locate the computer's expansion bus.

    Answer the following questions:

    How many free slots are in the computer?

    _____

    What types of slots are they?

    _____

    _____

5. Locate an appropriate bus slot for the NIC.

    In most cases, your NIC will require a Peripheral Component Interconnect (PCI) slot. If there are no slots of the appropriate type free in your computer, notify your instructor before continuing.

6. Remove the protective cover from the slot.

    The slot cover might have a Phillips-head screw holding it in place, or the computer might have some sort of hinged plate with a latch that holds all of the expansion boards and slot covers in place.

7. Remove the NIC from its antistatic bag and hold it over the slot you selected.

8. Line up the bus connector on the NIC with the bus slot in the computer.

9. Push down firmly on the top edge of the NIC to seat it fully into the slot.

   Different types of boards often require slightly different techniques to insert them into a slot. The bus connectors on Industry Standard Architecture (ISA) boards typically have rounded corners, enabling you to push the entire connector down into the slot at once. PCI boards typically have sharper corners, in which case it might be easier to hold the board at a slight angle and push one end of the connector into the slot first, and then the other end.

Note If you have problems inserting the board into the slot, ask your instructor for help. Expansion boards require firm pressure to seat them completely into the slot, but pushing down too firmly can damage the board or even crack the computer's motherboard.

---

10. Secure the NIC in the slot, using the mechanism provided.

11. Replace the cover on the computer case.

Exercise 3
Building the LAN

In this exercise, you will assemble the LAN by connecting both computers to the hub.

▶ **To connect the computers**

1. Shut down the workgroup server computer (if it is running).

2. Place the hub you examined in Exercise 1 in a location that is central to the two workgroup computers and close to a power outlet.

3. Plug the hub's power cord into the unit and into the power outlet.

   What happens to the LED indicators on the hub?

   _____

4. Take one of the UTP cables and plug one end into the NIC in the workgroup server.

5. Plug the other end of the cable into one of the hub's standard ports.

   What happens to the LED indicators on the hub and the NIC?

   _____

6. Take the other cable and plug one end into the hub's uplink port.

   If the uplink port is switched, make sure that the switch is in the uplink position.

7. Take the other end of the cable and plug it into the NIC you just installed into the workgroup workstation.

8. Plug the power cord back into the workstation computer and into a power outlet.

   What happens to the LED indicators on the hub and the NIC now?

   _____

9. Unplug the workstation's network cable from the uplink port in the hub and plug it into one of the standard ports.

   What happens to the LED indicators now?

   _____

Exercise 4
Understanding NIC Configuration

In this exercise, you will explore the configuration interface for the NIC.

▶   **To view the NIC configuration**

Note This exercise assumes that the NIC, the computer, and its basic input/output system (BIOS) all support the Plug and Play standard, so that no manual installation or configuration of the network adapter driver is necessary.

1. Press the power button on the workstation computer to start the machine.
2. When the Welcome To Windows screen appears, press CTRL+ALT+DEL.
3. In the User Name text box, type **Administrator** (if it is not there already); then in the Password text box, type the password for the computer (as supplied by your instructor), and then click OK.
4. Click Start, point to Settings, and then click Control Panel.
5. In Control Panel, double-click System, and then select the Hardware tab.
6. Click Device Manager to open the Device Manager dialog box.
7. Expand the Network Adapters heading.

    Notice that the NIC you installed in Exercise 2 has been automatically detected by Plug and Play and that a network adapter driver has been installed.

8. Select the name of the network interface adapter (or NIC) installed in the computer, and then on the Action menu, select Properties.

    The Properties dialog box for the network interface adapter appears.

    What message appears in the Device Status box on the General tab?

    _____

    _____

9. Select the Resources tab.

    This tab contains the hardware resource settings that the network adapter driver is configured to use. When Plug and Play detects the network interface adapter in the computer, it configures the adapter with specific resource settings and then installs the driver, configuring it to use those same settings.

    What interrupt request (IRQ) is the network adapter driver configured to use?

    _____

What input/output range is the network adapter driver configured to use?

_____

Is the network adapter driver configured to use any other resource settings? If yes, what are they?

_____

_____

10. Try to click the Change Setting button.

    What happens? Why?

    _____

    _____

11. Select the Advanced tab.

    This tab contains additional parameter settings that are specific to the NIC installed in the computer. These settings typically let you configure NIC performance features and do not affect the basic operation of the NIC.

12. Click OK to close the Properties dialog box.

13. Close the Device Manager window.

14. Log off the workgroup server and workgroup workstation.

Lab 3: Configuring TCP/IP

Objectives

After completing this lab, you will be able to

- Determine the Transmission Control Protocol/Internet Protocol (TCP/IP) configuration parameters that a computer running Microsoft Windows 2000 is currently using
- Install and remove the TCP/IP client on a computer running Windows 2000
- Configure the TCP/IP parameters on a computer running Windows 2000

Note Completing this lab will help reinforce your learning from Chapter 11 of the textbook.

Before You Begin

This lab assumes that the hardware configurations of your workgroup server and workstation have been left as they were at the end of Lab 2, with both computers connected to ports in the workgroup hub. The hub should not be connected to the classroom network at this time.

In addition to the equipment already provided, your instructor should provide you with a third network cable, as well as the following information:

- The password for the Administrator account on your workgroup server and workstation, assigned by your instructor
- The Internet Protocol (IP) addresses on the classroom network for the server and the workstation
- A subnet mask value for the classroom IP addresses
- The IP addresses for the server and for the workstation that uses a network address that is unique to that workgroup
- A subnet mask value for the workgroup IP addresses
- The IP address of the classroom server (or the address of another computer on the network running the DNS Server service)

Enter the information you are given in the following table:

Parameter	Workgroup Server	Workgroup Workstation
Classroom IP address	_____	_____
Classroom subnet mask	_____	_____
Workgroup IP address	_____	_____
Workgroup subnet mask	_____	_____
Classroom Domain Name System (DNS) server address	_____	_____

In this lab, you will work through a scenario in which you are a junior network support technician who is working at a remote site under the instruction of a supervisor on the telephone.

Estimated time to complete the lab: 30 minutes

Exercise 1
Viewing TCP/IP Configuration Parameters

As the new employee in the company's IS department, you are responsible for much of the legwork that needs to be done, such as traveling around the corporate campus to sites where problems are occurring. Today, you are at a remote building on the campus where a Windows 2000 workgroup has been malfunctioning. The TCP/IP configuration of the workgroup's two computers is suspected to be the cause. When you arrive at the site, you call your supervisor and are instructed to check what IP address and other TCP/IP configuration parameters the computers are using.

Note There are two ways to view the TCP/IP configuration parameters used by a computer running Windows 2000. You can open the Internet Protocol (TCP/IP) Properties dialog box or use the Ipconfig utility. Ipconfig is a simple utility that, when executed from the command prompt, displays the TCP/IP configuration parameters for the computer.

List the steps you would take to display your workgroup server's TCP/IP configuration, using Control Panel.

_____

_____

_____

_____

_____

_____

What can you tell about the computer's TCP/IP configuration from this dialog box?

_____

_____

To display your workgroup server's TCP/IP configuration using the Ipconfig utility, use the following procedure:

1. Log on to your workgroup server as Administrator, using the password supplied by your instructor.

2. Click Start, point to Programs, point to Accessories, and then click Command Prompt.

3. Type **ipconfig** at the prompt, and then press ENTER.

   What are the IP Address and Subnet Mask values for the computer, according to Ipconfig?

   _____

   _____

Note The computer was assigned this address by the Windows 2000 Automatic Private IP Addressing (APIPA) feature. When a computer running Windows 2000 is configured to obtain its TCP/IP settings using Dynamic Host Configuration Protocol (DHCP), and there is no DHCP server available on the network, the computer assigns itself an address from the range 169.254.0.1 to 169.254.255.254.

Exercise 2
Obtaining TCP/IP Configuration Parameters Using DHCP

Your supervisor tells you to check the workgroup server's network connectivity, using Windows Explorer. Describe the steps you would perform to do this.

_____

_____

_____

_____

What domains and workgroups do you see?

_____

What do you see when you expand the icon for your workgroup?

_____

Your supervisor now tells you to connect the two-computer workgroup network to the larger classroom network. To do this, connect your workgroup hub to the classroom network by plugging one end of your remaining network cable into the hub's uplink port and the other end into the classroom network jack. Wait a few moments, and then refresh the Windows Explorer display and check the computer's network connectivity again.

What has changed, now that you've connected the hub to the classroom network?

_____

Why can't you see the rest of the network?

_____

_____

_____

Your supervisor now tells you to refresh the DHCP client on the workgroup server in order to obtain a new IP address and other configuration parameters. To do this, use the following procedure:

1. Click Start, point to Programs, point to Accessories, and then click Command Prompt.
2. Type **ipconfig /renew** at the prompt, and then press ENTER.

The ipconfig /renew command causes the TCP/IP client to obtain configuration settings from the DHCP server on the classroom network and display them on the screen.

What are the IP Address and Subnet Mask values of the server now?

_____

_____

Refresh the DHCP client on the workgroup workstation in the same way.

What are the IP Address and Subnet Mask values of the workstation computer?

_____

_____

Exercise 3
Installing and Removing Protocols

Your supervisor is unsure whether the workgroup's communication difficulties are being caused by a TCP/IP configuration problem or a networking hardware problem. To determine whether the hardware is at fault, your supervisor tells you to install the NetBIOS Extended User Interface (NetBEUI) protocol on both of the computers in the workgroup and remove the TCP/IP clients entirely.

Note Installing NetBEUI on both computers can help to isolate the problem because the NetBEUI protocol requires no outside configuration. If the workgroup computers can communicate normally with NetBEUI instead of TCP/IP, then the networking hardware is definitely not at fault, and the problem lies somewhere in the TCP/IP configuration.

List the steps you will use to install the NetBEUI Protocol module and uninstall the Internet Protocol (TCP/IP) module on the workgroup computers. (Assume that you are already logged on to the workgroup workstation as Administrator.)

_____

_____

_____

_____

_____

_____

_____

_____

_____

_____

_____

After performing this procedure on both computers, use Windows Explorer again to check the workgroup's connectivity.

Can the two computers in the workgroup communicate with each other? Why or why not?

_____

_____

Can the workgroup computers see the rest of the classroom network? Why or why not?

_____

_____

Your supervisor is satisfied that the workgroup's problem is not being caused by the networking hardware. You now need to reverse the procedure you performed before by removing NetBEUI and installing TCP/IP again on both workgroup computers. List the steps to do this.

_____

_____

_____

_____

_____

_____

_____

_____

_____

_____

Exercise 4
Configuring the TCP/IP Client

The newly installed Internet Protocol (TCP/IP) modules on your workgroup computers are once again configured to use DHCP to obtain their TCP/IP configuration parameters. Your supervisor now decides to eliminate DHCP from the equation and configure the TCP/IP clients on the workgroup computers manually.

To start, your supervisor tells you to configure both the server and the workstation with IP addresses and subnet masks that are unique to the workgroup.

Using the information in the "Workgroup IP address" and "Workgroup subnet mask" rows of the table you filled out in the "Before You Begin" section of this lab, list the steps needed to configure the TCP/IP clients for the workgroup computers.

_____

_____

_____

_____

_____

_____

_____

_____

_____

_____

_____

Once you have configured both of the workgroup computers, your supervisor tells you to use the Windows 2000 Ping utility to test the connectivity between them by opening the Command Prompt window on the workgroup server, typing **ping** plus the workstation's IP address, and then pressing ENTER.

What is the result, and what does that result indicate?

_____

_____

Next, use the Ping utility to test the workgroup server's connectivity to the instructor's server, using the value you entered in the "Classroom DNS server address" row in the table (in the "Before You Begin" section of this lab).

What is the result? Why did you get that result?

_____

_____

_____

Now reconfigure the TCP/IP client on the workgroup server to use the classroom IP address and classroom subnet mask values from the table, and use the classroom DNS server address value to configure the server's Preferred DNS Server parameter. Then use the Ping utility to test the workgroup server's connectivity to the workgroup workstation and the instructor's server.

What happens? Why?

_____

_____

_____

List the steps you need to complete to configure the workgroup server so that it can communicate with both the workgroup workstation and the instructor's server.

_____

_____

_____

_____

_____

_____

_____

_____

_____

_____

Now repeat the ping test you performed earlier to test the connectivity both to the workgroup workstation and to the instructor's server.

What happens now? Why?

_____

_____

_____

Your supervisor is now satisfied that the computers in the workgroup are functioning properly with DHCP. Remove the manual TCP/IP settings on both the workgroup server and workstation and configure them to use DHCP again. Leave the hub connected to the classroom network, and log off the workgroup server and workgroup workstation.

Lab 4: Using NetWare Clients

Objectives

After completing this lab, you will be able to

- Install a NetWare client on a computer running Microsoft Windows 2000 Server or Advanced Server
- Configure Gateway Service for NetWare (GSNW) to share NetWare server resources
- Access NetWare resources with a computer running Windows 2000 that is not a NetWare client

---

Note Completing this lab will help reinforce your learning from Chapter 4 of the textbook.

Before You Begin

This lab assumes that the hardware and software configuration of your workgroup network is the same as it was at the end of Lab 3, with both computers connected to ports in the workgroup hub and the hub connected to the classroom network.

To complete this lab, you will need the following information:

- The password for the Administrator account on your workgroup server and workstation, assigned by your instructor.
- The password for the Administrator account on the classroom NetWare server, assigned by your instructor.
- The two-digit number assigned to your workgroup by your instructor. This number is used to form the name of your workgroup (WGxx, where xx is the number assigned to your workgroup) and your workgroup workstation (WGxxWrkstn). (You will use this value in this lab to calculate new Internet Protocol [IP] address and subnet mask values for your workgroup computers.)

Estimated time to complete the lab: 30 minutes

Exercise 1
Installing Gateway Service for NetWare

In this exercise, you will install the GSNW module on your workgroup server, enabling it to access NetWare resources.

▶ **To install GSNW**

1. Log on to your workgroup server as Administrator, using the password supplied by your instructor.

2. Click Start, point to Settings, and then click Network And Dial-Up Connections.

   The Network And Dial-Up Connections window appears.

3. Right-click the Local Area Connection icon, and then click Properties to open the Local Area Connection Properties dialog box.

   What networking components are currently installed on the computer?

   _____

   _____

   _____

4. Click Install.

5. In the Select Network Component Type dialog box, select Client, and then click Add.

6. In the Select Network Client dialog box, select Gateway (And Client) Services For NetWare, and then click OK.

   At this point, you might have to specify the location of the Microsoft Windows 2000 distribution files, located in the \Windist folder on drive C.

7. When the Local Network message box appears, click Yes to restart the computer.

Exercise 2
Configuring GSNW

In this exercise, you will configure the newly installed GSNW module to access the NetWare server and to share a NetWare volume.

▶   **To configure GSNW**

1. When the workgroup server has restarted, log on as Administrator, using the password supplied by your instructor.

   The Select NetWare Logon dialog box appears.

2. Click Default Tree And Context. In the Tree text box, type **NWTREE1** and in the Context text box, type **classroom** and then click OK.

Note The Preferred Server option is for use with NetWare servers that are not running Novell Directory Services (NDS), such as NetWare versions 3.2 and earlier.

---

3. Click Start, point to Settings, and then click Network And Dial-Up Connections.

   The Network And Dial-Up Connections window appears.

4. Right-click the Local Area Connection icon, and then click Properties to open the Local Area Connection Properties dialog box.

   What networking components appear in the Local Area Connection Properties dialog box now?

   _____

   _____

   _____

   _____

   Why were other modules in addition to the Gateway (And Client) Services for NetWare module installed at this time?

   _____

   _____

   _____

5. Click OK to close the Local Area Connection Properties dialog box.

6. Click Start, point to Programs, point to Accessories, and then click Windows Explorer.

   The Windows Explorer window appears.

7. Expand the My Network Places icon, and then expand Entire Network.

   What do you see?

   _____

   _____

8. Expand the NetWare Or Compatible Network icon.

   What icons appear and what do they represent?

   _____

   _____

9. Click Start, point to Settings, and then click Control Panel.

   The Control Panel window appears.

   Notice that the installation of Gateway (And Client) Services for NetWare added a GSNW icon to Control Panel.

10. Double-click the GSNW icon.

    The Gateway Service For NetWare dialog box appears.

    What are the functions of the Print Options check boxes?

    _____

    _____

    _____

    _____

11. Click Gateway.

    The Configure Gateway dialog box appears.

12. Select the Enable Gateway check box.

13. In the Gateway Account text box, type **Administrator**.

14. In the Password and Confirm Password text boxes, type the password to the Administrator account supplied by your instructor.

Note The gateway account is a user account in the NDS database (or in the NetWare bindery) that the NetWare server will use to access the files and folders shared by the GSNW service on the computer running Windows 2000. This account must be a member of an NDS (or bindery) group called NTGATEWAY and must have the appropriate permissions needed to access the files on the server that are to be shared. Your instructor has already created the appropriate user and group accounts on the NetWare server.

15. Click Add.

    The New Share dialog box appears.

16. In the Share Name text box, type **NW_SYS**.

    This is the name Microsoft Windows clients will use to access the shared NetWare files and folders.

17. In the Network Path text box, type **\\NW1\SYS**.

    This is the path to the volume on the NetWare server that you intend to share, expressed in the form \\server\volume.

18. In the Comment text box, type **NetWare SYS Volume**.

19. Use the default values for the Use Drive and User Limit settings, and then click OK to close the New Share dialog box.

    The Use Drive selector specifies the drive letter that will be assigned to the share on the computer running GSNW. The controls in the User Limit box let you limit the number of users who can access the shared NetWare volume through the gateway.

Warning It is not recommended that you use GSNW to support a large number of users who must make extensive use of NetWare resources for a long period of time. All of the NetWare traffic running through the Windows 2000 server can degrade performance in other areas.

20. Click OK to close the Configure Gateway dialog box.

21. Click OK to close the Gateway Service For NetWare dialog box.

Exercise 3
Accessing NetWare Resources

In this exercise, you will access the SYS volume on the NetWare server, using both the client capabilities of GSNW and the Windows client on your workgroup workstation.

▶ **To access NetWare resources**

1. On the workgroup server, click Start, point to Programs, point to Accessories, and then click Windows Explorer.

   The Window Explorer window appears.

2. Expand the My Network Places icon, the Entire Network icon, the NetWare Or Compatible Network icon, and the Nw1 icon.

   What icons do you see below the Nw1 icon, and what do they represent?

   _____

   _____

   _____

3. Create a new folder, WG*xx*, in the Sys volume, named for your workgroup (where *xx* is the number assigned to your workgroup by your instructor).

4. Copy the Eula.txt file from the C:\Windist folder on your server to the \WG*xx* folder you just created on the NetWare volume.

5. Log on to your workgroup workstation as Administrator.

6. At the workgroup workstation, click Start, point to Settings, and then click Network And Dial-Up Connections.

   The Network And Dial-Up Connections window appears.

7. Right-click the Local Area Connection icon, and then click Properties to open the Local Area Connection Properties dialog box.

   What networking components appear in the Local Area Connection Properties dialog box?

   _____

   _____

   _____

8. Click Start.

9. Click Start, and then click Run.

   The Run dialog box appears.

10. In the Open text box, type **\\WGxxSvr** and then press ENTER.

    What happens now?

    _____

    _____

    What shares do you see on the server?

    _____

    _____

11. Double-click the NW_SYS icon.

    The \\WGxxSvr\NW_SYS window appears.

    What do you see in this window?

    _____

12. Double-click the \WGxx folder.

    What do you see when you open the \WGxx folder?

    _____

    Explain how this is possible.

    _____

13. Log off the workgroup server and the workgroup workstation.

Lab 5: Using Directory Services

Objectives

After completing this lab, you will be able to

- Join a computer running Microsoft Windows 2000 to a domain
- Promote a computer running Microsoft Windows 2000 Server to a domain controller
- Access a Windows 2000 domain
- Remove a computer running Windows 2000 from a domain
- Demote a domain controller to a member server

Note Completing this lab will help reinforce your learning from Chapter 4 of the textbook.

Before You Begin

This lab assumes that your workgroup is still configured as it was at the end of Lab 4, with both computers connected to ports in the workgroup hub and the hub connected to the classroom network.

To complete this lab, you will need the following information:

- The password for the Administrator account on your workgroup server and workstation, assigned by your instructor.
- The password for the Administrator account on the Instructor01 classroom server, assigned by your instructor.
- The two-digit number assigned to your workgroup by your instructor. This number is used to form the name of your workgroup (WG*xx*, where *xx* is the number assigned to your workgroup) and your workgroup workstation (WG*xx*Wrkstn).
- The password for the Instructor01 server, assigned by your instructor.

Estimated time to complete the lab: 45 minutes

Exercise 1
Joining a Domain

In this exercise, you will join your workgroup server to the classroom domain in preparation for promoting it to a domain controller.

▶ **To join a domain**

1. Log on to your workgroup server as Administrator, using the password supplied by your instructor.
2. Click Start, point to Settings, and then click Control Panel.

   The Control Panel window appears.
3. Double-click the System icon.
4. In the System Properties dialog box, select the Network Identification tab.
5. Click Properties.

   The Identification Changes dialog box appears.

   What is the name of the workgroup the computer belongs to?

   _____

6. In the Identification Changes dialog box, click the Domain button. Then, in the Domain text box, type **contoso.msft** and then click OK.

   The Domain Username And Password dialog box appears.
7. In the Name text box, type **Administrator**; in the Password text box, type the password supplied by your instructor for the Administrator account on the Instructor01 classroom server; and then click OK.

   What happens now?

   _____

   _____

8. Click OK.

   Another Network Identification message box appears, informing you that you must restart the computer.
9. Click OK.
10. Click OK again to close the System Properties dialog box.
11. Click Yes to restart the computer.

Exercise 2
Creating a Domain Controller

In this exercise, you will promote your workgroup server to a domain controller, creating a new child domain off the classroom domain.

▶ **To promote a server to a domain controller**

1. Log on to your workgroup server as Administrator, using the password supplied by your instructor.

Note Do not log on to the domain you just joined.

2. Click Start, and then click Run.

   The Run dialog box appears.

3. In the Open text box, type **dcpromo** and then click OK.

   The Active Directory Installation Wizard is launched.

4. Click Next to bypass the Welcome page.

   The Domain Controller Type page appears.

5. Make sure that Domain Controller For A New Domain is selected, and then click Next.

   The Create Tree Or Child Domain page appears.

6. Select Create A New Child Domain In An Existing Domain Tree, and then click Next.

   The Network Credentials page appears.

7. In the User Name text box, type **Administrator** and then in the Password text box, type the password for the Administrator account on the Instructor01 classroom server supplied by your instructor.

   What appears in the Domain text box?

8. Click Next.

   The Child Domain Installation page appears. The Parent Domain text box should already contain Contoso.msft.

9. In the Child Domain text box, type the name of your workgroup, **WG*xx*** (where *xx* is the number assigned to your workgroup by your instructor) and then click Next.

   The NetBIOS Domain Name page appears.

   The name of your workgroup should appear in the Domain NetBIOS Name text box.

10. Click Next.

    The Database And Log Locations page appears.

11. Leave the default values in place on the Database And Log Locations page, and then click Next.

    The Shared System Volume page appears.

12. Leave the default value in place on the Shared System Volume page, and then click Next.

    The Permissions page appears.

13. Leave the default value in place on the Permissions page, and then click Next.

    The Directory Services Restore Mode Administrator Password page appears.

14. In the Password and Confirm Password text boxes, type the password for the Administrator account on your workgroup server supplied by your instructor, and then click Next.

    The Summary page appears.

15. Review the information presented on the Summary page, and then click Next.

    The wizard proceeds to install the Active Directory service and create the new child domain.

Note This procedure might take several minutes.

Note If an Active Directory Installation Wizard message box appears, stating "As part of the promotion process, this server was disjoined from its domain," click OK to continue.

16. On the Completing The Active Directory Installation Wizard page, click Finish.

    An Active Directory Installation Wizard message box appears, informing you that you must restart the computer.

17. Click Restart Now.

18. When the workgroup server has restarted, log on again as Administrator, using the password supplied by your instructor.

Exercise 3
Accessing a Domain

In this exercise, you will join your workgroup workstation to the new domain you have created and log on to the new domain.

▶ **To access the new domain**

1. Log on to your workgroup workstation as Administrator, using the password supplied by your instructor.

2. Click Start, point to Settings, and then select Control Panel.

   The Control Panel window appears.

3. Double-click the System icon.

4. In the System Properties dialog box, select the Network Identification tab.

5. Click Properties.

   The Identification Changes dialog box appears.

6. Click the Domain button.

7. In the Domain text box, type **WGxx** (where *xx* is the number assigned to your workgroup by your instructor), and then click OK.

   The Domain Username And Password dialog box appears.

8. In the Name text box, type **Administrator;** in the Password text box, type the password for the Administrator account on the workgroup server supplied by your instructor; and then click OK.

   A Network Identification message box appears, welcoming you to the WGxx domain.

9. Click OK.

   A Network Identification message box appears, informing you that you must restart the computer.

10. Click OK.

11. Click OK again to close the System Properties dialog box.

12. Click Yes to restart the computer.

13. Once the workstation restarts, press CTRL+ALT+DEL to display the Log On To Windows dialog box.

14. If necessary, click Options to expand the dialog box so that the Log On To drop-down list appears.

   What options appear in the Log On To drop-down list?

   _____

   _____

   _____

15. In the Log On To drop-down list, select WG*xx*; in the User Name text box, leave Administrator; in the Password text box, type the password for the Administrator account on the workgroup server supplied by your instructor, and then click OK to log on to the domain.

16. Click Start, point to Programs, point to Accessories, and then click Windows Explorer.

   The Windows Explorer window appears.

17. Expand the My Network Places icon and the Entire Network icon, and then click the Directory icon.

   What icon do you see, and what does it represent?

   _____

   _____

18. Expand the Contoso icon.

   Now what icons do you see, and what do they represent?

   _____

   _____

   _____

   _____

19. Close Windows Explorer.

Exercise 4
Removing a Domain

In this exercise, you will return your computers to their original workgroup configuration by removing the computers from their domains, uninstalling Active Directory, and deleting the child domain you created.

▶ **To demote a domain controller**

1. On the workstation computer, click Start, point to Settings, and then click Control Panel.

2. Double-click the System icon.

   The System Properties dialog box appears.

3. Select the Network Identification tab.

4. Click Properties.

   The Identification Changes dialog box appears.

5. Click the Workgroup option button; then in the Workgroup text box, type your workgroup name (WG*xx*, where *xx* is the number assigned to your workgroup by your instructor); and then click OK.

   A Network Identification message box appears, welcoming you to the WG*xx* workgroup.

6. Click OK.

   Another Network Identification message box appears, informing you that you must restart the computer for the changes you made to take effect.

7. Click OK.

8. Click OK again to close the System Properties dialog box.

9. Click Yes to restart the computer.

10. At the workgroup server, log on to the Contoso.msft domain as Administrator, using the password for the Instructor01 server supplied by your instructor.

Note If the Enter Password dialog box appears, type the password for the Administrator account on the classroom NetWare server in the Password text box, and then click OK.

11. On the workgroup server, click Start, and then click Run.

    The Run dialog box appears.

12. In the Open text box, type **dcpromo** and then click OK.

    The Active Directory Installation Wizard is launched.

13. Click Next to bypass the Welcome page.

    The Remove Active Directory page appears.

14. Select the This Server Is The Last Domain Controller In The Domain check box, and then click Next.

    The Network Credentials page appears.

15. In the User Name text box, type **Administrator**; in the Password text box, type the password for the Instructor01 server supplied by your instructor (Contoso.msft should already appear in the Domain text box); and then click Next.

    The Administrator Password page appears.

16. In the Password and Confirm Password text boxes, type the password for the Administrator account on the workgroup server supplied by your instructor, and then click Next.

    The Summary page appears.

17. Review the information on the Summary page, and then click Next.

    The wizard proceeds to uninstall Active Directory and remove the domain.

Note This procedure might take several minutes.

---

18. Click Finish, and then click Restart Now to restart the computer.

19. Log on to the workgroup server as Administrator, using the password supplied by your instructor, and repeat steps 1–8 of this exercise to rejoin it to your workgroup.

20. After restarting the system, open Windows Explorer and then expand the My Network Places and Entire Network icons.

    What has changed? Why?

    _____

    _____

    _____

21. Close Windows Explorer.

22. Log off the workgroup server and workgroup workstation.

Lab 6: Analyzing Data-Link Layer Protocols

Objectives

After completing this lab, you will be able to

- Capture Ethernet traffic from your network
- Examine the contents of Ethernet packets

Note Completing this lab will help reinforce your learning from Chapter 5 of the textbook.

Before You Begin

This lab assumes that your workgroup is still configured as it was at the end of Lab 5, with both computers connected to ports in the workgroup hub and the hub connected to the classroom network. The workgroup server should still have the Network Monitor application installed and configured, as detailed in Lab 1, and Gateway Service for NetWare (GSNW) should still be installed and operational, as outlined in Lab 4.

To complete this lab, you will need the following information:

- The password for the Administrator account on your workgroup server and workstation, assigned by your instructor.
- The two-digit number assigned to your workgroup by your instructor. This number is used to form the name of your workgroup (WG*xx*, where *xx* is the number assigned to your workgroup), your workgroup server (WG*xx*Svr), and your workgroup workstation (WG*xx*Wrkstn).

Estimated time to complete the lab: 30 minutes

Exercise 1
Generating and Capturing Traffic

In this exercise, you will create network traffic using the computers in your workgroup and then capture a sample for analysis.

▶ **To generate network traffic**

1. Log on to your workgroup workstation as Administrator, using the password supplied by your instructor.

2. Click Start, point to Programs, point to Accessories, and then click Windows Explorer.

3. Copy the \Windist folder on drive C to the \WGxx folder (where xx is the number assigned to your workgroup by your instructor) in the NW_SYS share that you created in Lab 4.

   Windows Explorer begins copying the contents of the \Windist folder (which contains over 300 MB of Microsoft Windows 2000 distribution files) to the \WGxx folder on the NW_SYS share.

Note The process of copying the Windows 2000 distribution files to the NW_SYS share should take 10 minutes or more, depending on the speed of your network and your computers. You must perform several of the steps in the next procedure while the copy process is proceeding.

▶ **To capture network traffic**

1. Log on to your workgroup server as Administrator, using the password supplied by your instructor.

2. Click Start, point to Programs, point to Administrative Tools, and then click Network Monitor.

3. On the Network Monitor Capture menu, select Start to begin capturing network traffic.

   Watch the % Buffer Utilized indicator on the right side of the screen.

4. When the % Buffer Utilized indicator reaches 100%, select Stop And View from the Capture menu.

   The Capture Window appears, containing a list of the packets you just captured.

5. Return to your workgroup workstation and abort the file copy procedure you initiated in the previous procedure.

6. Back on the server, examine the values that appear in the Src MAC Addr, Dst MAC Addr, Src Other Addr, and Dst Other Addr columns in the Capture Window.

What form do these values take?

_____

_____

To facilitate the protocol analysis process in the next exercise, you should replace any Internet Protocol (IP) addresses that appear in these columns with computer names. List the steps for a procedure that will accomplish this.

_____

_____

_____

_____

_____

_____

_____

_____

_____

Exercise 2
Analyzing Ethernet Traffic

In this exercise, you will examine the contents of the Ethernet packets you captured in the previous exercise.

▶   **To analyze captured packets**

1. With the Capture Window in Network Monitor displayed, select Filter from the Display menu.

    The Display Filter dialog box appears.

2. Double-click the Protocol == Any entry.

    The Expression dialog box appears.

3. With the Protocol tab selected, click Disable All.

    The entries in the Enabled Protocols list are moved to the Disabled Protocols list.

4. Scroll down the Disabled Protocols list and select the NBT (NetBIOS Over TCP/IP) entry.

5. Click Enable.

    The NBT entry appears in the Enabled Protocols list.

6. Click OK to close the Expression dialog box.

7. Click OK to close the Display Filter dialog box.

    What happens to the Capture Window? Why?

    _____

    _____

    _____

Note As noted in Lab 1, applying a display filter specifying one particular protocol causes Network Monitor to display all of the packets using that protocol in any way. Applying the NBT filter will normally result in the display of SMB packets, because SMB uses NBT as its underlying protocol.

---

8. Double-click one of the packets in the Capture Window.

    The detail and hex panes appear, containing information about the selected packet.

9. In the detail pane, double-click the plus sign (+) next to the Ethernet entry. What is the ETYPE value of the packet?

_____

What does this value mean?

_____

_____

_____

What can you tell about the frame format from this information?

_____

_____

What is the value of the Destination Address field in the packet you selected?

_____

What is the name of the destination computer identified by this address?

_____

How can you tell?

_____

_____

10. Open the Display Filter dialog box again and double-click the Protocol == NBT entry.

   The Expression dialog box appears.

11. Click Disable All.

   NBT is removed from the Enabled Protocols list.

12. Scroll down the Disabled Protocols list and and select the NCP (NetWare Core Protocol) entry.

13. Click Enable.

   The NCP entry appears in the Enabled Protocols list.

14. Click OK to close the Expression dialog box.

15. Click OK to close the Display Filter dialog box.

    What happens to the Capture Window now?

    _____

    _____

    Why do these packets appear in the capture?

    _____

    _____

    _____

    _____

16. Select one of the packets in the Capture Window to displays its contents in the detail and hex panes.

    What Ethernet frame format is the packet using?

    _____

    What is the Ethertype value of this packet?

    _____

    How does the Ethernet frame identify the protocol that generated the data in the packet?

    _____

    _____

    What field replaces the Ethertype field in the IEEE 802.3 packet?

    _____

17. Close Network Monitor, clicking No when asked if you want to save the capture.

18. Log off the workgroup server and the workgroup workstation.

Lab 7: Analyzing Network Layer Protocols

Objectives

After completing this lab, you will be able to

- Capture Internet Protocol (IP), Internet Packet Exchange (IPX), and NetBIOS Extended User Interface (NetBEUI) traffic from your network
- Analyze the network layer protocols
- Understand the functions of the header fields in the network layer protocols

---

Note Completing this lab will help reinforce your learning from Chapter 6 of the textbook.

Before You Begin

This lab assumes that your workgroup is still configured as it was at the end of Lab 6, with both computers connected to ports in the workgroup hub and the hub connected to the classroom network. The workgroup server should still have the Network Monitor application installed and configured, as detailed in Lab 1, and Gateway Service for NetWare (GSNW) should still be installed and operational, as outlined in Lab 4.

To complete this lab, you will need the following information:

- The password for the Administrator account on your workgroup server and workstation, assigned by your instructor.
- The two-digit number assigned to your workgroup by your instructor. This number is used to form the name of your workgroup (WG*xx*, where *xx* is the number assigned to your workgroup), your workgroup server (WG*xx*Svr), and your workgroup workstation (WG*xx*Wrkstn).

Estimated time to complete the lab: 45 minutes

Exercise 1
Capturing IP and IPX Traffic

In this exercise, you will generate IP and IPX traffic on your workgroup network simultaneously, using the same procedure you used in Lab 6, and capture a sample of it using Network Monitor.

▶   **To capture IP and IPX traffic**

1. Log on to your workgroup workstation as Administrator, using the password supplied by your instructor.

2. On the workgroup workstation, click Start, point to Programs, point to Accessories, and then click Windows Explorer.

3. Copy the \Windist folder on drive C to the \WG*xx* folder in the NW_SYS share that you created in Lab 4 (where *xx* is the number assigned to your workgroup), overwriting the existing files as needed.

4. Log on to your workgroup server as Administrator, using the password supplied by your administrator.

5. On the workgroup server, click Start, point to Programs, point to Administrative Tools, and then click Network Monitor.

6. On the Network Monitor Capture menu, select Start to begin capturing network traffic.

    Watch the % Buffer Utilized indicator on the right side of the screen.

7. When the % Buffer Utilized indicator reaches 100%, select Stop And View from the Capture menu.

    The Capture Window appears, containing a list of the packets you just captured.

8. Return to your workgroup workstation and abort the file copy procedure.

Exercise 2
Analyzing IP Traffic

In this exercise, you will apply a display filter to the network traffic sample you just captured in Exercise 1 and examine the IP datagrams.

▶ **To examine the IP datagrams**

1. At your workgroup server, with the Capture Window in Network Monitor open, select Filter from the Display menu.

   The Display Filter dialog box appears.

2. Double-click the Protocol == Any entry.

   The Expression dialog box appears.

3. With the Protocol tab open, click Disable All.

   The entries in the Enabled Protocols list are moved to the Disabled Protocols list.

4. Scroll down the Disabled Protocols list and select the IP (Internet Protocol) entry.

5. Click Enable.

   The IP (Internet Protocol) entry appears in the Enabled Protocols list.

6. Click OK to close the Expression dialog box.

7. Click OK to close the Display Filter dialog box.

   What happens to the Capture Window?

   _____

   _____

   What is the benefit of this step?

   _____

   _____

8. Double-click one of the packets in the Capture Window.

   The detail and hex panes appear, containing information about the selected packet.

9. In the detail pane, double-click the plus sign (+) next to the IP entry.

10. Double-click the plus sign next to the Flags Summary entry.

11. Examine the contents of the IP header, and then answer the following questions.

What version of IP is the computer using?

_____

Under what conditions could the value of the Version field be different?

_____

_____

What is the length of the IP header in the packet you are studying?

_____

What does this header length signify?

_____

_____

How much data (in bytes) is being carried in the datagram?

_____

How can you tell?

_____

_____

Has the datagram you are studying been fragmented?

_____

How can you tell?

_____

_____

Why has the datagram not been fragmented?

_____

_____

What is the default Time To Live value set by computers running Microsoft Windows?

_____

What is the Time To Live value for the packet you are studying?

_____

Why are both values the same?

_____

_____

Exercise 3
Analyzing IPX Traffic

In this exercise, you will modify the display filter to show only the IPX traffic in the captured traffic sample and then analyze the IPX packets.

▶   **To analyze the IPX traffic**

1. With the Capture Window in Network Monitor open, select Filter from the Display menu.

    The Display Filter dialog box appears.

2. Double-click the Protocol == Any entry.

    The Expression dialog box appears.

3. With the Protocol tab open, click Disable All.

    The entries in the Enabled Protocols list are moved to the Disabled Protocols list.

4. Scroll down the Disabled Protocols list and select the IPX (Internet Packet Exchange) entry.

5. Click Enable.

    The IP (Internet Packet Exchange) entry appears in the Enabled Protocols list.

6. Click OK to close the Expression dialog box.

7. Click OK to close the Display Filter dialog box.

    What happens to the Capture Window?

    _____

    _____

8. In the detail pane, double-click the plus signs next to the IPX, Destination Address Summary, and Source Address Summary entries. Then answer the following questions.

    Is there a network layer error detection mechanism in the packet, and if so, what field implements it?

    _____

    _____

    How much data is being carried in the IPX datagram?

    _____

How can you tell?

_____

_____

What is the value of the Transport Control field?

_____

Why is this so?

_____

_____

_____

What is the value given in the Destination Address Summary entry?

_____

What is the significance of this value?

_____

_____

_____

9. On the File menu, select Save As.

10. In the Save As dialog box, type **ip-ipx.cap** in the File Name text box, and then click Save.

11. Close the Capture Window containing the traffic sample.

Exercise 4
Capturing and Analyzing NetBEUI Traffic

In this exercise, you will install the NetBEUI protocol on your workgroup computers, capture a traffic sample, and analyze the NetBEUI Frame protocol.

▶   **To analyze NetBEUI traffic**

1. On the workgroup server, click Start, point to Settings, and then click Network And Dial-Up Connections.

2. Right-click the Local Area Connection icon, and then select Properties.

3. Click Install.

4. Select Protocol, and then click Add.

5. Select NetBEUI Protocol, and then click OK.

6. Click Close.

7. On the workgroup workstation, repeat steps 1–5 to install the NetBEUI protocol.

8. On the workgroup workstation, in the Local Area Connection Properties dialog box, select Internet Protocol (TCP/IP), and then click Uninstall.

   An Uninstall Internet Protocol (TCP/IP) message box appears, informing you that uninstalling the protocol removes it from all network connections.

9. Click Yes.

   A Local Network message box appears, informing you that you must restart the computer for the changes you have made to take effect.

10. Click Yes to restart the computer.

11. When the workstation restarts, log on again as Administrator, using the password supplied by your instructor.

12. Launch Windows Explorer.

13. Expand the My Network Places, Entire Network, Microsoft Windows Network, WG*xx,* and WG*xx*Svr icons (where *xx* is the number assigned to your workgroup), and then click the C share icon.

14. Copy the \Windist folder on the workgroup server to the root of drive C on the workstation, overwriting the existing files as needed.

15. On the workgroup server, in Network Monitor, select Start from the Capture menu.

16. When a Save File message box appears, asking if you want to save the capture, click No.

17. When the % Buffer Utilized indicator reaches 100%, select Stop And View from the Capture menu.

18. Return to your workgroup workstation and abort the file copy procedure.

19. On the workgroup server, study the Capture screen in Network Monitor.

    How does this packet capture summary differ from the others you have seen?

    _____

    _____

20. Scroll down the frame list and locate a Data Only Last packet (as shown in the Description column).

21. Double-click the packet to display the detail and hex panes.

22. In the detail pane, double-click the plus (+) sign next to the NetBIOS entry.

    Study the information that is displayed and then answer the following questions.

    What is the total size of the NBF datagram (header and data)?

    _____

    How do you know?

    _____

    _____

    What is the value of the Response Correlator field?

    _____

23. In the summary pane, locate the next Data Ack packet following the Data Only Last packet you just studied, and then select it to study its contents.

    What is the value of the Transmit Correlator field?

    _____

    How does this value compare with the Response Correlator value in the previous packet?

    _____

Explain the relationship between the two fields.

_____

_____

_____

_____

Note The remaining steps in this procedure are simply for restoring TCP/IP on the workgroup workstation.

24. Close Network Monitor, clicking No when asked if you want to save the capture.

25. On the workgroup workstation, click Start, point to Settings, and then click Network And Dial-Up Connections.

26. Right-click the Local Area Connection icon, and then select Properties.

27. Click Install.

28. Select Protocol, and then click Add.

29. Select Internet Protocol (TCP/IP), and then click OK.

30. Click Close.

31. Log off the workgroup server and the workgroup workstation.

Lab 8: Analyzing Transport Layer Protocols

Objectives

After completing this lab, you will be able to

- Capture Transmission Control Protocol (TCP) and User Datagram Protocol (UDP) traffic from your network
- Analyze the transport layer protocols
- Understand the functions of the header fields in the transport layer protocol

---

Note Completing this lab will help reinforce your learning from Chapter 7 of the textbook.

Before You Begin

This lab assumes that your workgroup is still configured as it was at the end of Lab 7, with both computers connected to ports in the workgroup hub and the hub connected to the classroom network. The workgroup server should still have the Network Monitor application installed and configured, as detailed in Lab 1.

To complete this lab, you will need the following information:

- The password for the Administrator account on your workgroup server and workstation, assigned by your instructor.
- The two-digit number assigned to your workgroup by your instructor. This number is used to form the name of your workgroup (WG*xx*, where *xx* is the number assigned to your workgroup), your workgroup server (WG*xx*Svr), and your workgroup workstation (WG*xx*Wrkstn).

Estimated time to complete the lab: 30 minutes

Exercise 1
Capturing TCP Traffic

In this exercise, you will generate TCP traffic on your workgroup network by giving your workstation access to the Administration Web site on the server and connecting to it using Microsoft Internet Explorer.

Note You do not need an Internet connection to complete this procedure.

▶ **To capture TCP traffic**

1. Log on to your workgroup server as Administrator, using the password supplied by your instructor.

2. Click Start, point to Programs, point to Administrative Tools, and then click Internet Services Manager.

3. In the left pane of the Internet Information Services console, expand the icon for your server, right-click the Administration Web Site icon, and then click Properties.

4. In the Web Site tab of the Administration Web Site Properties dialog box, note the value of the TCP Port field and write it in the space below.

---

5. Select the Directory Security tab, and then, in the IP Address And Domain Name Restrictions box, click Edit.

6. In the IP Address And Domain Name Restrictions dialog box, click Granted Access, and then click OK.

7. Click OK to close the Administration Web Site Properties dialog box.

8. Close the Internet Information Services console.

9. Click Start, point to Programs, point to Administrative Tools, and then click Network Monitor.

10. In the Network Monitor window, on the Capture menu, select Start to begin capturing network traffic.

11. Log on to your workgroup workstation as Administrator, using the password supplied by your instructor.

12. On the workgroup workstation, click Start, point to Programs, and then click Internet Explorer to launch the Internet Connection Wizard.

13. On the Welcome To The Internet Connection Wizard page, click I Want To Set Up My Internet Connection Manually, and then click Next.

14. On the Setting Up Your Internet Connection page, click I Connect Through A Local Area Network (LAN), and then click Next.

15. On the Local Area Network Internet Configuration page, clear the Automatic Discovery Of Proxy Server (Recommended) check box, and then click Next.

16. On the Set Up Your Internet Mail Account page, click No, and then click Next.

17. On the Completing The Internet Connection Wizard page, click Finish.

18. When Internet Explorer opens, type **http://WG*xx*Svr:####** in the Address box (where *xx* is the number assigned to your workgroup by your instructor and **####** is the TCP Port value you noted earlier in this exercise), and then press ENTER.

    A Microsoft Internet Explorer message box appears, warning you that you are not using a secure connection.

19. Click OK.

20. Return to the server and, on the Network Monitor Capture menu, select Stop And View.

Exercise 2
Analyzing TCP Traffic

In this exercise, you will apply a display filter to the network traffic sample you just captured, and then you will examine the TCP headers.

▶ **To examine TCP traffic**

1. With the Capture Window in Network Monitor displayed, on the Display menu, select Filter.

   The Display Filter dialog box appears.

2. Double-click the Protocol == Any entry.

   The Expression dialog box appears.

3. In the Protocol tab, click Disable All.

   The entries in the Enabled Protocols list are moved to the Disabled Protocols list.

4. Scroll down the Disabled Protocols list and select the TCP (Transmission Control Protocol) entry.

5. Click Enable.

   The TCP entry appears in the Enabled Protocols list.

6. Click OK to close the Expression dialog box.

7. Click OK to close the Display Filter dialog box.

   What happens to the Capture Window?

   _____

   _____

8. In the capture summary, locate a packet that contains SYN as its only control bit, and then double-click it to display the detail and hex panes.

   Notice that the value in the Description column for each TCP packet begins with a summary of the control bits in that packet, using their first initials.

9. Double-click the TCP entry in the detail pane to display the message header information. Then answer the following questions.

   What is the function of this packet?

   _____

   _____

What is the maximum segment size (MSS) specified by your workgroup workstation?

_____

How can you tell?

_____

_____

What is the workstation's initial sequence number (ISN) value for this connection?

_____

How do you know?

_____

_____

What is the workstation's Acknowledgment Number value in this packet?

_____

Why is the Acknowledgment Number value what it is?

_____

_____

Without looking at the Network Monitor screen, what is the Acknowledgment Number value in the server's SYN/ACK message?

_____

How can you tell without looking?

_____

_____

What is the ISN supplied to the workstation by the server?

_____

Based on this information and without looking at the Network Monitor screen, what will the Sequence Number and Acknowledgment Number values be for the workstation's ACK message that concludes the handshake?

_____

How can you predict these values?

_____

_____

_____

_____

10. Scroll down the summary list and locate the next connection termination sequence.

   How can you tell which packets are used to terminate a TCP connection?

   _____

   _____

   Without looking at the Network Monitor screen, can you tell for certain which computer initiated the termination sequence? Why or why not?

   _____

   _____

   Now look at the Network Monitor screen. Which computer initiated the termination sequence?

   _____

   Why is this the case?

   _____

   _____

11. Close the Capture Window.

Exercise 3
Analyzing UDP Traffic

In this exercise, you will use the Nslookup utility to generate UDP traffic and capture it using Network Monitor. Then you will analyze the contents of the UDP header.

▶ **To analyze UDP traffic**

1. In Network Monitor on the workgroup server, select Start from the Capture menu.

2. When a Save File message box appears, asking if you want to save the capture (from Exercise 2), click No.

3. Click Start, point to Programs, point to Accessories, and then click Command Prompt.

4. In the Command Prompt window, type **nslookup instructor01** and then press ENTER.

5. When the program finishes displaying its response, type **exit** in the Command Prompt window, and then press ENTER.

6. Return to Network Monitor and select Stop And View from the Capture menu.

7. Select Filter from the Display menu.

   The Display Filter dialog box appears.

8. Double-click the Protocol == Any entry.

   The Expression dialog box appears.

9. With the Protocol tab displayed, click Disable All.

   The entries in the Enabled Protocols list are moved to the Disabled Protocols list.

10. Scroll down the Disabled Protocols list and select the UDP (User Datagram Protocol) entry.

11. Click Enable.

    The UDP entry appears in the Enabled Protocols list.

12. Click OK to close the Expression dialog box.

13. Click OK to close the Display Filter dialog box.

14. Double-click the first Domain Name System (DNS) protocol packet appearing in the summary window.

15. In the detail pane, double-click the UDP entry to display the contents of the UDP header. Then answer the following questions.

Which computer generated the packet you are examining?

_____

Which computer received the packet?

_____

What is the packet's Destination Port value?

_____

What does this value mean?

_____

_____

_____

What is the value of the message's Source Port field?

_____

What does this value represent?

_____

_____

16. Scroll down the summary window to the next DNS message on which your workgroup server is the destination system.

Without looking at the Network Monitor screen, what is the Source Port value for this message?

_____

How can you tell?

_____

_____

_____

What is the value of the Destination Port field?

_____

Where did this value come from?

_____

_____

17. Close Network Monitor, clicking No when asked if you want to save the capture.

18. Log off the workgroup server and the workgroup workstation.

Lab 9: Calculating IP Addresses

Objectives

After completing this lab, you will be able to

- Create a subnet
- Calculate a subnet mask
- Determine the Internet Protocol (IP) addresses to use on a subnetted network

---

Note Completing this lab will help reinforce your learning from Chapter 8 of the textbook.

Before You Begin

This lab assumes that your workgroup is still configured as it was at the end of Lab 8, with both computers connected to ports in the workgroup hub and the hub connected to the classroom network.

To complete this lab, you will need the following information:

- The password for the Administrator account on your workgroup server and workstation, assigned by your instructor.
- The two-digit number assigned to your workgroup by your instructor. This number is used to form the name of your workgroup (WG*xx*, where *xx* is the number assigned to your workgroup), your workgroup server (WG*xx*Svr), and your workgroup workstation (WG*xx*Wrkstn).

Estimated time to complete the lab: 30 minutes

Exercise 1
Converting Binaries to Decimals

In this exercise, you will learn how to convert a binary value into a decimal value. This is an important skill to master before learning to create subnets and calculate subnet masks and IP addresses.

▶ **To convert a binary number to a decimal**

IP addresses consist of 32 bits, broken up into four 8-bit values. When you subnet a network, the subnet mask bits you borrow from the host identifier do not always fall on the boundary between octets. As a result, you often have to use a subnet mask in which an octet has mixed network identifier and host identifier bits. To use this type of mask, you must know how to convert the binary value for the octet into a decimal value.

For example, take a network with a Class B address, such as 172.28.0.0. You have learned that the default subnet mask for a Class B address is 255.255.0.0. In binary form, the mask appears as follows:

```
11111111 11111111 00000000 00000000
```

This type of value is easy to convert, because you know that the binary value of zero is also zero, and the binary value of 11111111 is 255. However, if you decide to take five bits from the host identifier for use as a subnet identifier, the subnet mask changes. In binary form, this change is easy to see:

```
11111111 11111111 11111000 00000000
```

To convert this value into a usable subnet mask, you know that the first and second octets still have a value of 255, and the last octet still has a value of 0. However, the third octet now has a binary value of 11111000. To convert this value into a decimal, you must assign a decimal value to each of the eight digits, starting at the right with 1 and doubling the value for each digit as you move to the left. The decimal equivalents for the digits of an 8-bit value therefore appear as follows:

```
128    64    32    16    8    4    2    1
```

To convert the binary value 11111000, you add the decimal values for each binary bit with a value of 1, as follows:

```
128    64    32    16    8    4    2    1
  1     1     1     1    1    0    0    0

128 + 64 + 32 + 16 + 8              = 248
```

You calculate that the value for the third octet in the given subnet mask is 248. The value for the entire mask is 255.255.248.0.

Using this method, calculate the decimal equivalents for the following subnet masks, and write the values in the corresponding spaces below.

```
11111111 11000000 00000000 00000000
```

_____

```
11111111 11111111 11111111 11110000
```

_____

```
11111111 11111100 00000000 00000000
```

_____

```
11111111 11111111 11100000 00000000
```

_____

There are also times during the subnetting process when you must convert octet values where the 1 bits are not consecutive. Using the same method as before, convert the following binary octet values into decimal form.

```
00110111
```

_____

```
10100001
```

_____

```
11111001
```

_____

```
00001110
```

_____

Exercise 2
Calculating a Subnet Mask

In this exercise, you will calculate the subnet mask value needed to connect your workgroup server to the classroom network.

▶   **To calculate a subnet mask**

Your instructor has given you the network address used to configure the IP address on the classroom server Instructor01, as well as the number of subnet identifier bits used to subnet the network address.

Your instructor has reconfigured the IP address on the classroom server Instructor01 by creating a subnet for a given network address. The IP address you are going to use is 10.0.64.xx (where xx is the number your instructor has assigned to your workgroup). Write the full IP address for your workgroup server in the space below.

_____

In which IP address class is the address you have been given?

_____

How can you tell the class of the address?

_____

When reconfiguring the IP address of the classroom server, your instructor created a subnet using 10 bits borrowed from the host identifier. Assuming that the subnet identifier used for the classroom network has a decimal value of 1, write the binary value for the subnet identifier in the space below.

_____

Using this information, calculate the subnet mask value you must use on your workgroup server to connect to the classroom network and access the Instructor01 server. Write the subnet mask in the space below.

_____

Next, use the following procedure to configure your workgroup server with this IP address and subnet mask.

1. Log on to your workgroup server as Administrator, using the password supplied by your instructor.
2. Click Start, point to Settings, and then click Network And Dial-Up Connections.
3. Right-click the Local Area Connection icon, and then select Properties.
4. Select Internet Protocol (TCP/IP) in the list of components, and then click Properties.
5. Select Use The Following IP Address.
6. Type the IP address you noted above in the IP Address box.
7. Type the subnet mask value you just calculated in the Subnet Mask box.
8. Click OK to close the Internet Protocol (TCP/IP) Properties dialog box.
9. Click OK to close the Local Area Connection Properties dialog box.

Next, open the Command Prompt window and use the Ping utility to test your connection to the classroom server.

What command should you use to do this?

If you have calculated the subnet mask value correctly, the ping test should be successful.

Exercise 3
Creating a Subnet

In this exercise, you are given a network address value and a number of subnet identifier bits. You will use this information to create a unique subnet for your workgroup and configure your computers with the appropriate IP addresses and subnet masks.

▶   **To create a subnet**

For this exercise, you will use the network address 192.168.16.0 and create a subnet using five of the host identifier bits as a subnet identifier. What class is this network address?

_____

Which octet of the IP addresses you calculate will contain the subnet identifier bits?

_____

Calculate the subnet mask you will use for this network, using the method shown in the previous exercises, and write it in the space below.

_____

The value of the subnet identifier for your IP addresses should be the same value assigned to your workgroup by your instructor. To determine the binary value for the subnet identifier, you can count in binary up to your decimal workgroup number. For example, if your decimal workgroup number is 06, the equivalent 5-bit binary value would be 00110. The binary values for the decimal numbers 1 through 10 are given in the following table.

Decimal	Binary
1	00001
2	00010
3	00011
4	00100
5	00101
6	00110
7	00111
8	01000
9	01001
10	01010

Write the binary value for your subnet identifier in the space below.

_____

After allocating 5 bits for your subnet identifier, how many bits are left for the host identifier?

_____

Using a decimal value of 1 for your workgroup server and 2 for your workgroup workstation, what are the binary values you will use for your host identifiers?

_____

Now write the binary value for the entire fourth octet of your workgroup server's IP address in the space below.

_____

Convert the binary fourth octet value to a decimal and write the complete IP address for your workgroup server in the space below.

_____

Use the same method to calculate the IP address for the workgroup workstation and write it in the space below.

_____

Finally, disconnect your hub from the classroom network and use the procedure in Exercise 2 to configure your workgroup server and workstation with the IP addresses and subnet mask you calculated in this exercise. If your calculations are correct, your workgroup computers should be able to communicate with each other normally.

Log off the workgroup server and the workgroup workstation.

Lab 10: Using TCP/IP Applications

Objectives

After completing this lab, you will be able to

- Install and configure a Dynamic Host Configuration Protocol (DHCP) server on a computer running Microsoft Windows 2000
- Capture DHCP traffic and analyze it
- Renew a DHCP lease

Note Completing this lab will help reinforce your learning from Chapter 10 of the textbook.

Before You Begin

This lab assumes that your workgroup is still configured as it was at the end of Lab 9, with both computers connected to ports in the workgroup hub and the hub disconnected from the classroom network. The workgroup server should still have the Network Monitor application installed and configured, as detailed in Lab 1.

To complete this lab, you will need the following information:

- The password for the Administrator account on your workgroup server and workstation, assigned by your instructor.
- The two-digit number assigned to your workgroup by your instructor. This number is used to form the name of your workgroup (WG*xx*, where *xx* is the number assigned to your workgroup), your workgroup server (WG*xx*Svr), and your workgroup workstation (WG*xx*Wrkstn).
- The Internet Protocol (IP) address and subnet mask that you calculated and configured your workgroup workstation to use in Exercise 3 of Lab 9.

Estimated time to complete the lab: 30 minutes

Exercise 1
Installing DHCP

In this exercise, you will install and configure the DHCP Server service on your workgroup server.

▶   **To install and configure DHCP**

1. Log on to your workgroup server as Administrator, using the password supplied by your instructor.

2. Click Start, point to settings, and then select Control Panel.

3. Double-click the Add/Remove Programs icon in Control Panel to open the Add/Remove Programs dialog box.

4. Click Add/Remove Windows Components to open the Windows Components Wizard.

5. Select Networking Services in the Components list, and then click Details to open the Networking Services dialog box.

6. Select the check box next to the Dynamic Host Configuration Protocol (DHCP) entry in the Subcomponents Of Networking Services list, and then click OK to return to the Windows Components Wizard.

7. Click Next to install the DHCP Server service.

8. Click Finish to complete the installation and close the Windows Components Wizard.

9. Click Close to close the Add/Remove Programs dialog box.

10. Click Start, select Shut Down, and then restart the computer to initialize DHCP.

11. Log on again as Administrator.

12. Click Start, point to Programs, and select DHCP from the Administrative Tools program group to open the DHCP console.

13. Select the entry for your DHCP server in the scope (left) pane, and then select New Scope from the Action menu to open the New Scope Wizard.

14. Click Next to bypass the Welcome page and proceed to the Scope Name page.

15. Type **Workgroup WG*xx* Scope** in the Name box (where *xx* is the number assigned to your workgroup), and then click Next.

16. In the Start IP Address box, type an IP address that consists of the address you assigned to your workgroup workstation in Exercise 3 of Lab 9, plus 1.

    For example, if your workstation IP address was 192.168.16.18, use the value 192.168.16.19 for this field.

17. In the End IP Address box, type your workstation IP address from Exercise 3 of Lab 9, plus 4.

    For example, if your workstation IP address was 192.168.16.18, use the value 192.168.16.22 for this field.

18. In the Subnet Mask box, type **255.255.255.248** and then click Next.

19. Click Next to bypass the Add Exclusions page.

20. On the Lease Duration page, specify a lease duration of 5 minutes, and then click Next.

21. On the Configure DHCP Options page, select No, I Will Configure These Options Later, and then click Next.

22. Click Finish to create the scope and close the wizard.

23. In the DHCP console, select the scope you just created, and then select Activate from the Action menu.

24. Select the icon for your server in the left pane of the DHCP console.

    What do you see in the right pane?

    _____

Exercise 2
Capturing DHCP Traffic

In this exercise, you will generate DHCP traffic on your workgroup network and capture it with Network Monitor.

▶   **To capture DHCP traffic**

1. On the workgroup server, click Start, point to Programs, point to Administrative Tools, and then click Network Monitor.

2. On Network Monitor's Capture menu, select Start to begin capturing network traffic.

3. Log on to your workgroup workstation as Administrator, using the password supplied by your instructor.

4. On the workgroup workstation, click Start, point to Settings, and then click Network And Dial-Up Connections.

5. Right-click the Local Area Connection icon.

6. Select Internet Protocol (TCP/IP) in the list of components, and then click Properties.

7. Select Obtain An IP Address Automatically, and then click OK.

8. Click OK to close the Internet Protocol (TCP/IP) Properties dialog box.

9. Click Start, select Shut Down, and then restart the computer.

   Why is it necessary to restart the computer at this time?

   _____

10. When the workstation restarts, log on again as Administrator.

11. After waiting a minute or so to be sure the DHCP sequence is complete, move to the workgroup server, and on the Network Monitor Capture menu, select Stop And View.

12. On the Display menu, select Filter.

13. Select the Protocol == Any entry, and then click Edit Expression.

14. In the Expression dialog box, click Disable All.

15. Scroll down the Disabled Protocols list and select DHCP (Dynamic Host Configuration Protocol) from the Name column, and then click Enable.

16. Click OK to close the Expression dialog box.

17. Click OK to close the Display Filter dialog box.

   The Capture Summary window now contains only the DHCP messages in the traffic sample.

18. Double-click the first Discover message that appears in the capture summary to display the detail and hex panes.

19. In the detail pane, double-click the plus sign (+) next to the DHCP entry to view the contents of the message.

    What is the IP address used by the DHCP client in the Discover message?

    _____

    Why is this value used?

    _____

20. In the summary pane, locate the Offer message that follows the Discover message, and then click it.

21. Double-click the plus sign next to the DHCP entry to view the contents of the message.

22. Double-click the plus (+) sign next to the DHCP Option Field entry.

    How can you tell for certain that this Offer message has been sent in reply to the Discover message?

    _____

    What IP address has the server offered to the client?

    _____

    How can you tell?

    _____

    How long after the IP address is assigned to the client will the client attempt to renew the lease?

    _____

    How can you tell for certain?

    _____

    Did the workstation accept the address offered by the server? How can you tell (without looking at the workstation computer)?

    _____

Exercise 3
Renewing a Lease

In this exercise, you will renew an IP address lease and view the messages involved.

▶   **To renew a lease**

1. In Network Monitor on the workgroup server, close the Capture Window, and then select Start from the Capture menu to start the program capturing traffic again.

2. When a Save File message box appears, click No.

3. On the workgroup workstation, click Start, point to Programs, point to Accessories, and then click Command Prompt.

4. In the Command Prompt window, type **ipconfig /all** and then press ENTER.

   What IP address is the workstation currently using?

   _____

   What time was the current lease obtained?

   _____

5. At the command prompt, type **ipconfig /release** and then press ENTER.

6. When the command prompt returns, type **ipconfig /all** again and then press ENTER.

   What IP address is the workstation using now? Why?

   _____

7. Type **ipconfig /renew** and then press ENTER.

   What IP address is the workstation using now?

   _____

8. Type **ipconfig /all** and then press ENTER.

   When was the current lease obtained?

   _____

9. On the workgroup server, select Stop And View from the Capture menu.

10. Repeat steps 13–18 in Exercise 2 to configure the display filter to show only DHCP traffic.

    What types of DHCP messages appear in the capture summary?

    _____

    _____

11. Close the Capture Window (without saving the file), and then select Start from the Capture menu to start Network Monitor capturing traffic again.

12. Wait three minutes.

13. Select Stop And View from the Capture menu.

14. Repeat steps 13–18 in Exercise 2 to configure the display filter to show only DHCP traffic.

    What DHCP messages significant to this process appear in the traffic sample?

    _____

    Why were these messages generated?

    _____

15. Log off the workgroup server and the workgroup workstation.

Lab 11: Making Network Connections

Objectives

After completing this lab, you will be able to

- Install a second network interface adapter in a computer running Microsoft Windows 2000

- Configure a computer running Microsoft Windows 2000 Server to function as a router

---

Note Completing this lab will help reinforce your learning from Chapter 3 of the textbook.

Before You Begin

This lab assumes that your workgroup is still configured as it was at the end of Lab 10, with both computers connected to ports in the workgroup hub and the hub disconnected from the classroom network. The workgroup server is running the DHCP Server service. The workgroup workstation is configured as a Dynamic Host Configuration Protocol (DHCP) client and is using an Internet Protocol (IP) address leased from the server.

To complete this lab, you will need the following hardware:

- A second Plug and Play network interface adapter (referred to in this lab as a network interface card, or NIC) to install in the workgroup server

- One unshielded twisted-pair (UTP) network cable

- Tools for working on the computer (if needed)

- Static control equipment (antistatic wrist straps or mats)

You will also need the following information:

- The password for the Administrator account on your workgroup server and workstation, assigned by your instructor.

- The two-digit number assigned to your workgroup by your instructor. This number is used to form the name of your workgroup (WG*xx*, where *xx* is the number assigned to your workgroup), your workgroup server (WG*xx*Svr), and your workgroup workstation (WG*xx*Wrkstn).

- The IP address and subnet mask that you calculated and configured your workgroup workstation to use in Exercise 3 of Lab 9.

Estimated time to complete the lab: 30 minutes

Exercise 1
Installing a Second NIC

In this exercise, you will install a second NIC in your workgroup server so that you can connect it to two different networks and configure it to function as a router.

► **To install a second NIC**

1. Shut down the workgroup server computer (if it is running), and unplug the power cable from the back of the case.

2. Prepare your work area by setting up the antistatic equipment you have been provided.

Caution Always perform these first two safety steps before working inside any computer.

3. Remove the cover from the case and set it aside.

Tip Most computers use thumbscrews, plastic latches, or both to hold the case onto the computer. On older machines, you may have to remove a number of Phillips-head screws to open the case.

4. Locate the computer's expansion bus and find an appropriate bus slot for the NIC.

   In most cases, your NIC will require a Peripheral Component Interconnect (PCI) slot. If there are no slots of the appropriate type free in your computer, notify your instructor before continuing.

5. Remove the protective cover from the slot.

Tip The slot cover might have a Phillips-head screw holding it in place, or the computer might have some sort of hinged plate with a latch that holds all of the expansion cards and slot covers in place.

6. Remove the NIC from its antistatic bag and hold it over the slot you selected.

7. Line up the bus connector on the NIC with the bus slot in the computer.

8. Push down firmly on the top edge of the NIC to seat it fully into the slot.

Tip Different types of cards often require slightly different techniques to insert them into a slot. The bus connectors on Industry Standard Architecture (ISA) cards typically have rounded corners, so you can push the entire connector down into the slot at once. PCI cards typically have sharper corners, so it might be easier to hold the card at a slight angle and first push one end of the connector into the slot, and then the other end.

Note If you have problems inserting the card into the slot, ask your instructor for help. Expansion cards require firm pressure to seat them completely into the slot, but pushing down too firmly can damage the card or even crack the computer's motherboard.

9. Secure the NIC in the slot, using the mechanism provided.

10. Replace the cover on the computer case.

11. Use the UTP cable to connect the computer to the classroom network, using the NIC you just installed.

Exercise 2
Connecting to Two Networks

In this exercise, you will see how installing a second NIC enables your workgroup server to connect to two networks.

▶ **To connect to two networks**

1. Plug the power cord into the workgroup server computer, and then turn on the computer.

2. When the computer has finished booting, log on as Administrator, using the password supplied by your instructor.

3. Click Start, point to Programs, point to Accessories, and then click Command Prompt.

4. In the Command Prompt window, type **ipconfig /all** and then press ENTER.

   What is the IP address assigned to the NIC that appears as the Local Area Connection in the Ipconfig display?

   _____

   Where did the computer get this IP address?

   _____

   _____

   What is the IP address assigned to the NIC you just installed (this address should appear in the Ipconfig display as Local Area Connection 2)?

   _____

   Where did this IP address come from?

   _____

   _____

5. At the command prompt, type **ping Instructor01** and then press ENTER.

   What happens?

   _____

6. Log on to your workgroup workstation, using the password supplied by your instructor.

7. Now test the connectivity to your workgroup workstation by typing **ping WGxxWrkstn** (where *xx* is the number assigned to your workgroup) and then pressing ENTER.

What happens?

_____

Why are both of these ping tests successful?

_____

_____

8. Move to the workgroup workstation and log on as Administrator, using the password supplied by your instructor.

9. Click Start, point to Programs, point to Accessories, and then click Command Prompt.

10. In the Command Prompt window, type **ipconfig /all** and then press ENTER.

What IP address is assigned to the NIC in the workstation?

_____

11. In the Command Prompt window, type **ping WGxxSvr** and then press ENTER.

What happens?

_____

Which NIC in the workgroup server is the workstation using to connect?

_____

How can you tell?

_____

_____

12. Now test the connectivity to the classroom server by typing **ping Instructor01** and then pressing ENTER.

What happens?

_____

13. Try connecting to the classroom server by typing **ping** plus the classroom server's IP address (which was displayed when you pinged it using the workgroup server) and then pressing ENTER.

What happens now?

_____

_____

Why did you receive the results you did?

_____

_____

_____

_____

Why were the results of the two attempts to ping the classroom server different?

_____

_____

_____

_____

Exercise 3
Installing Routing and Remote Access

In this exercise, you will configure your multihomed workgroup server to function as a router connecting your workgroup network to the classroom network.

▶ **To install Routing and Remote Access**

1. On the workgroup server, click Start, point to Programs, point to Administrative Tools, and then click Routing And Remote Access.

2. In the Routing And Remote Access console, click the icon for your server in the left pane, and then, from the Action menu, select Configure And Enable Routing And Remote Access.

   The Routing And Remote Access Server Setup Wizard is launched.

3. Click Next to bypass the Welcome page.

4. On the Common Configurations page, select Network Router, and then click Next.

5. Click Next to bypass the Routed Protocols page.

6. Click Next to bypass the Demand-Dial Connections page.

7. Click Finish to close the wizard.

8. Log off the workgroup server and the workgroup workstation.

Lab 12: Understanding TCP/IP Routing

Objectives

After completing this lab, you will be able to

- Create static routes on a computer running Microsoft Windows 2000
- Install the Routing Information Protocol (RIP)
- Capture and analyze RIP traffic

Note Completing this lab will help reinforce your learning from Chapter 9 of the textbook.

Before You Begin

This lab assumes that your workgroup is still configured as it was at the end of Lab 11, with a second network interface adapter installed in the workgroup server and Routing and Remote Access installed and configured, so that the server can function as a router between the workgroup network and the classroom network. The workgroup server should also still have the Network Monitor application installed and configured, as detailed in Lab 1.

To complete this lab, you will need the following information:

- The password for the Administrator account on your workgroup server and workstation, assigned by your instructor.
- The two-digit number assigned to your workgroup by your instructor. This number is used to form the name of your workgroup (WG*xx*, where *xx* is the number assigned to your workgroup), your workgroup server (WG*xx*Svr), and your workgroup workstation (WG*xx*Wrkstn).
- The Internet Protocol (IP) address of the Instructor01 server on the classroom network.
- The network address of one or more of the other workgroups in the classroom and the IP addresses of the computers in those workgroups.

Before you begin the lab, log on to both of your workgroup computers as Administrator, using the password supplied by your instructor, and use the ipconfig /all command to view the Transmission Control Protocol/Internet Protocol (TCP/IP) configuration parameters for both computers. Copy the following table on a separate sheet of paper and fill it out with the information displayed by IPCONFIG.EXE, and then give it to your instructor.

Workgroup number (assigned by your instructor)	
Workgroup server IP address (workgroup interface)	
Workgroup server IP address (classroom interface)	
Workgroup workstation IP address	

Your instructor will provide your information to one or more of the other workgroups in the classroom and will provide you with the same information for their computers.

Estimated time to complete the lab: 30 minutes

Exercise 1
Creating a Static Route with ROUTE.EXE

In this exercise, you will use the ROUTE.EXE program to create a static route that enables your workstation to communicate with the classroom network.

▶ **To create static routes**

1. On the workgroup workstation, click Start, and then click Run to open the Run dialog box.

2. Type **notepad c:\winnt\system32\drivers\etc\hosts** in the Open text box, and then click OK.

   The Microsoft Notepad application appears, with the contents of the Hosts file displayed.

3. At the bottom of the Hosts file, type the IP address for the Instructor01 server, press TAB, and then type **Instructor01**.

4. On the File menu, click Exit. When a Notepad message box appears, click Yes to save your changes.

5. Click Start, point to Programs, point to Accessories, and then click Command Prompt.

6. In the Command Prompt window, type **ping WG*xx*Svr** (where *xx* is the number assigned to your workgroup), and then press ENTER.

   Is the ping test successful? Why or why not?

   _____

   _____

7. Type **ping Instructor01** and then press ENTER.

   Is this ping test successful? How can you tell?

   _____

   _____

8. At the command prompt, type **ROUTE ADD 0.0.0.0 MASK 0.0.0.0** ***xxx.xxx.xxx.xxx*** (where *xxx.xxx.xxx.xxx* is the IP address of your workgroup server's interface to the workgroup network, listed in the table you filled out earlier).

9. Type **ping Instructor01** again in the Command Prompt window, and then press ENTER.

What are the results now?

_____

_____

What have you done to achieve these results?

_____

_____

_____

Exercise 2
Creating Static Routes with Routing and Remote Access

In this exercise, you will use the Routing And Remote Access console to create static routes on your workgroup server that enable the computers in your workgroup to access the other workgroup networks in the classroom. To complete this exercise, you must have a copy of the table like the one at the beginning of this lab, filled out by the members of another workgroup in the classroom.

► **To create static routes with the Routing And Remote Access console**

1. On the workgroup workstation, click Start, point to Programs, point to Accessories, and then click Command Prompt.

2. At the command prompt, type **ping** *xxx.xxx.xxx.xxx* (where *xxx.xxx.xxx.xxx* is the workgroup workstation IP address value from the table you have been given).

   What are the results of the ping test?

   _____

   _____

   Why did these results occur?

   _____

   _____

3. Log on to your workgroup server as Administrator, using the password supplied by your instructor.

4. Click Start, point to Programs, point to Administrative Tools, and then click Routing And Remote Access.

5. In the left pane of the Routing And Remote Access console, expand the icon for your server and the IP Routing icon.

6. Click Static Routes, and then select New Static Route on the Action menu.

7. In the Interface drop-down list, select the interface connecting your server to the classroom network (typically Local Area Connection 2).

8. In the Destination text box, type the workgroup server IP address (workgroup interface) value from the table you have been given, minus 1.

For example, if the address given in the table is 192.168.16.17, type
192.168.16.16 in the Destination text box.

Note The value you just entered in the Destination text box is the network
address of the other workgroup network. In Lab 9, each workgroup computed the
IP addresses for their computers and assigned the first address in the subnet to
the workgroup server. Therefore, the workgroup server address minus 1 is the
network address for that workgroup.

---

9. Type **255.255.255.248** in the Network Mask text box.

10. In the Gateway text box, type the workgroup server IP address (classroom
    interface) value from the table you have been given.

11. Click OK.

12. Return to your workgroup workstation and repeat the ping test in step 3.

    Why should the test now be successful?

    _____

    _____

Note If the ping test is unsuccessful, it is likely to be because the students in the
other workgroup have not yet finished creating a static route to your workgroup
network. Wait a few minutes and try again, or check on the progress of the other
group.

---

13. When the ping test has been successfully completed by both workgroups,
    select the static route you created in the right pane of the Routing And
    Remote Access console, and then select Delete on the Action menu.

Exercise 3
Installing the Routing Information Protocol

In this exercise, you will configure Routing and Remote Access to use RIP instead of static routes.

▶ **To install RIP**

1. Log on to your workgroup server as Administrator (if necessary), using the password supplied by your instructor.

2. Click Start, point to Programs, point to Administrative Tools, and then click Routing And Remote Access.

3. In the left pane of the Routing And Remote Access console, expand the icon for your server and the IP Routing icon.

4. Click General, and then select New Routing Protocol on the Action menu.

5. In the New Routing Protocol dialog box, select RIP Version 2 For Internet Protocol, and then click OK.

   The RIP icon appears under the IP Routing icon.

6. Click the RIP icon, and then select New Interface on the Action menu.

7. In the New Interface For RIP Version 2 For Internet Protocol dialog box, select the interface connecting the computer to the classroom network (typically Local Area Connection 2), and then click OK.

   The RIP Properties dialog box appears.

8. Click OK to close the RIP Properties dialog box.

9. Click Start, point to Programs, point to Administrative Tools, and then click Network Monitor.

10. On the Capture menu, select Networks.

11. In the Select A Network dialog box, expand Local Computer, select the entry corresponding to the classroom network interface, and then click OK.

Tip If necessary, use the ipconfig /all command in the Command Prompt window to display the hardware addresses for your computer's network interfaces, which Network Monitor lists in the Select A Network dialog box.

---

12. Select Start on the Capture menu to begin capturing network traffic.

13. Wait five minutes or until you know that the other workgroups in the classroom have had RIP running for several minutes, and then select Stop And View on the Capture menu.

14. Select Filter on the Display menu.

   The Display Filter dialog box appears.

15. Double-click the Protocol == Any entry.

    The Expression dialog box appears.

16. With the Protocol tab selected, click Disable All.

    The entries in the Enabled Protocols list are moved to the Disabled Protocols list.

17. Scroll down the Disabled Protocols list and select the RIP entry.

18. Click Enable.

    The RIP entry appears in the Enabled Protocols list.

19. Click OK to close the Expression dialog box.

20. Click OK to close the Display Filter dialog box.

    How many different routers have sent RIP response packets over the network?

    _____

21. Double-click a RIP Response packet, expand the RIP entry in the detail pane, and then expand the RIP: Data Frame entry.

22. Examine the contents of several RIP response packets and answer the following questions.

    What is the subnet mask value for the routing table entries arriving at the server?

    _____

    What is the highest value in the Metric field? Why?

    _____

    _____

23. In the Routing And Remote Access console, click Static Routes in the left pane, and then select Show IP Routing Table on the Action menu.

    How many new entries have been added to the routing table?

    _____

    How is using RIP an improvement over static routing?

    _____

    _____

24. Log off the workgroup server and the workgroup workstation.

Lab 13: Accessing Remote Networks

Objectives

After completing this lab, you will be able to

- Configure Microsoft Windows 2000 to function as a virtual private network (VPN) server
- Configure a VPN client
- Capture and analyze VPN traffic

Note Completing this lab will help reinforce your learning from Chapter 12 of the textbook.

Before You Begin

This lab assumes that your workgroup is still configured as it was at the end of Lab 12, with Routing and Remote Access installed and configured on the workgroup server so that the server can function as a router between the workgroup network and the classroom network. The workgroup server should also still have the Network Monitor application installed and configured, as detailed in Lab 1.

To complete this lab, you will need the following information:

- The password for the Administrator account on your workgroup server and workstation, assigned by your instructor.
- The two-digit number assigned to your workgroup by your instructor. This number is used to form the name of your workgroup (WG*xx*, where *xx* is the number assigned to your workgroup), your workgroup server (WG*xx*Svr), and your workgroup workstation (WG*xx*Wrkstn).

Estimated time to complete the lab: 30 minutes

Exercise 1
Configuring a VPN Server

In this exercise, you will modify the configuration of the Routing and Remote Access Service to allow remote network connections and to enable the Point-to-Point Tunneling Protocol (PPTP).

▶ **To configure a VPN server**

1. Log on to your workgroup server as Administrator, using the password supplied by your instructor.

2. Click Start, point to Programs, point to Administrative Tools, and then click Routing And Remote Access.

3. In the left pane of the Routing And Remote Access console, click the icon for your server, and then select Properties on the Action menu.

4. In the General tab of the server's Properties dialog box, select the Remote Access Server check box.

5. Select the IP tab, and then select the Allow IP-Based Remote Access And Demand-Dial Connections check box.

6. Click OK to close the Properties dialog box.

   A Routing And Remote Access message box appears, informing you that the router must be restarted in order for your configuration changes to take effect.

7. Click Yes to restart the router.

   The router takes a few seconds to restart.

8. In the left pane of the console, click the Ports icon, and then select Properties on the Action menu.

9. In the Ports Properties dialog box, click the WAN Miniport (PPTP) entry in the Devices list, and then click Configure.

10. In the Configure Device – WAN Miniport (PPTP) dialog box, select the Remote Access Connections (Inbound Only) check box, and then click OK.

11. Click OK to close the Ports Properties dialog box.

12. Click Start, point to Settings, and then click Network And Dial-Up Connections.

13. Right-click the Incoming Connections icon, and then click Properties.

14. Select the Users tab, select the Administrator check box in the Users Allowed To Connect list, and then click OK.

Exercise 2
Configuring a VPN Client

In this exercise, you will configure your workgroup workstation to function as a VPN client so that you can connect to the Routing and Remote Access Service on the workgroup server. Although you will be connecting to a server on the same local area network (LAN), the process is identical when connecting to a remote server through the Internet.

▶ **To configure a VPN client**

1. Log on to the workgroup workstation as Administrator, using the password supplied by your instructor.

2. Click Start, point to Settings, and then select Network And Dial-Up Connections.

3. In the Network And Dial-Up Connections window, double-click the Make New Connection icon to launch the Network Connection Wizard.

Note If there is a modem installed in your computer, a Location Information dialog box will appear, prompting you for your area code. Type your area code, and then click OK. Click OK again to close the Phone And Modem Options dialog box.

---

4. Click Next to bypass the Welcome page.

5. On the Network Connection Type page, select Connect To A Private Network Through The Internet, and then click Next.

6. On the Destination Address page, in the Host Name Or IP Address text box, type **WGxxSvr** (where *xx* is the number assigned to your workgroup), and then click Next.

7. Click Next to use the default setting on the Connection Availability page.

8. Click Next to bypass the Internet Connection Sharing page.

9. Click Finish to create the connection and close the Network Connection Wizard.

   A Connect Virtual Private Connection dialog box appears. You will come back to this dialog box in the next exercise.

Exercise 3
Connecting to a VPN Server

In this exercise, you will establish a connection between the VPN client on your workgroup workstation and the Routing and Remote Access Service on your workgroup server, while using Network Monitor to capture the traffic generated by the process.

▶   **To establish a VPN connection**

1. On the workgroup server, click Start, point to Programs, point to Administrative Tools, and then click Network Monitor.

2. On the Capture menu, select Networks.

3. In the Select A Network dialog box, expand Local Computer and select the entry corresponding to the workgroup network interface, and then click OK.

Tip If necessary, use the ipconfig /all command in the Command Prompt window to display the hardware addresses for your computer's network interfaces, which Network Monitor lists in the Select A Network dialog box.

---

4. On the Capture menu, select Start to begin capturing network traffic.

5. On the workgroup workstation, in the Connect Virtual Private Connection dialog box, in the Password text box, type the password for the Administrator account (supplied by your instructor) on the workgroup server, and then click Connect.

   A Connecting Virtual Private Connection status box appears as the client connects to the server. Then a Connection Complete message box appears.

6. Select the Do Not Display This Message Again check box, and then click OK.

7. On the workgroup server, on Network Monitor's Capture menu, select Stop And View.

8. Locate the first PPTP packet in Network Monitor's capture summary and double-click it to display the detail and hex panes containing the packet's contents.

   What transport layer protocol is carrying the PPTP messages?

   _____

   Judging from the information in the detail pane, at what layer of the Open Systems Interconnection (OSI) reference model is PPTP operating? How do you know?

   _____

After the series of PPTP message exchanges between the server and the workstation, what is the next protocol that Network Monitor shows them as using to communicate?

_____

What is the usual function of this protocol?

_____

_____

9. Click one of the messages using this protocol. In the following space, list all of the protocols used to carry that message, in order from the bottom of the protocol stack to the top.

_____

_____

What is unusual about the order of the protocols in this arrangement?

_____

_____

Exercise 4
Reconfiguring the Workgroup Network

In this exercise, you will disable the router on the workgroup server and return the workgroup network to its original configuration.

▶ **To reconfigure the workgroup network**

1. Click Start, point to Programs, point to Administrative Tools, and then click Routing And Remote Access.

2. In the left pane of the Routing And Remote Access console, click the icon for your server, and then select Disable Routing And Remote Access on the Action menu.

3. In the Routing And Remote Access message box, click Yes to continue.

4. Click Start, point to Settings, and then click Network And Dial-Up Connections.

5. In the Network And Dial-Up Connections window, click the Local Area Connection icon, and then select Properties on the File menu.

6. In the Local Area Connection Properties dialog box, click Internet Protocol (TCP/IP), and then click Properties.

7. In the Internet Protocol (TCP/IP) Properties dialog box, click Obtain An IP Address Automatically and, if necessary, click Obtain DNS Server Address Automatically, and then click OK.

8. Click OK again to close the Local Area Connection Properties dialog box.

9. In the Network And Dial-Up Connections window, right-click the Local Area Connection 2 icon, and then click Disable.

   This disables the connection for the second network interface adapter that you installed in an earlier lab.

10. Repeat steps 4–8 on the workgroup workstation.

11. Unplug the network cable connecting your server to the classroom network from the computer and plug it into the uplink port of your workgroup hub.

   This should leave you with your original workgroup network configuration, where both computers are plugged into the hub and the hub is connected to the classroom network.

12. Log off the workgroup server and the workgroup workstation.

Lab 14: Implementing Network Security Policies

Objectives

After completing this lab, you will be able to

- Set password policies on a computer running Microsoft Windows 2000
- Create a local user account
- Specify an appropriate password

Note Completing this lab will help reinforce your learning from Chapter 13 of the textbook.

Before You Begin

This lab assumes that your workgroup is still configured as it was at the end of Lab 13, with the workgroup server and workstation connected to the workgroup hub and the hub connected to the classroom network.

To complete this lab, you will need the following information:

- The password for the Administrator account on your workgroup server, assigned by your instructor

Estimated time to complete the lab: 20 minutes

Exercise 1
Setting Password Policies

In this exercise, you will configure your workgroup server to require passwords of a specific length and complexity.

▶   **To set password policies**

1. Log on to your workgroup server as Administrator, using the password supplied by your instructor.

2. Click Start, point to Programs, point to Administrative Tools, and then click Local Security Policy.

3. In the left pane of the Local Security Settings console, expand the Account Policies folder, and then select the Password Policy folder beneath it.

4. In the right pane of the console, double-click the Minimum Password Length policy.

5. In the Local Security Policy Setting dialog box, in the Local Policy Setting box, set the minimum password length to 8 characters, and then click OK.

6. Double-click the Maximum Password Age policy, set it to 7 days, and then click OK.

7. Double-click the Minimum Password Age policy, set it to 1 day, and then click OK.

8. Double-click the Passwords Must Meet Complexity Requirements policy, select Enabled, and then click OK.

9. Restart the computer.

Exercise 2
Creating a User Account

In this exercise, you will create a new user account for your workgroup, and then you will test the password settings for that account, as you specified them in Exercise 1.

▶ **To create a user account**

1. Log on to your workgroup server as Administrator, using the password supplied by your instructor.

2. Click Start, point to Programs, point to Administrative Tools, and then select Computer Management.

3. Expand the System Tools icon in the left pane of the console, and then expand Local Users And Groups beneath it.

4. Click the Users folder, and then select New User on the Action menu.

5. In the New User dialog box, type **tkim** in the User Name text box.

6. In the Full Name text box, type **Tim Kim**.

7. Type **newuser** in the Password text box and again in the Confirm Password text box.

Note Be sure to type all Windows 2000 passwords exactly as shown, including capitalization.

---

8. Make sure that the User Must Change Password At Next Logon check box is selected, and then click Create.

   What happens?

   _____

9. Click OK to return to the New User dialog box.

10. Type **Newuser1** in the Password text box and again in the Confirm Password text box, and then click Create.

    What happens now?

    _____

11. In the New User dialog box, click Close.

12. On the workgroup server, click Start, click Shut Down, select Log Off Administrator from the drop-down list, and then click OK.

13. Log on to the workgroup server as the user **tkim**, using the **Newuser1** password you assigned to the account.

    What happens?

    _____

14. Click OK to continue.

15. In the Change Password dialog box, type **tkim1** in the New Password text box and again in the Confirm New Password text box, and then click OK.

    A Change Password message box appears, informing you that the password you supplied is unacceptable. Why is this so?

    _____

16. Click OK.

    The Change Password dialog box reappears.

17. In the Old Password text box, type **Newuser1**; then type **timkim11** in the New Password text box and again in the Confirm New Password text box, and then click OK.

    What happens? Why is this password unacceptable?

    _____

18. Click OK, and type **Newuser1** in the Old Password text box; then type **WinUser1** in the New Password text box and again in the Confirm New Password text box, and then click OK.

    A message box appears, informing you that your password has been changed. Why is this password acceptable?

    _____

19. Click OK.

    A Logon Message box appears, informing you that your password will expire in 7 days and asking if you want to change it now.

20. Click No.

21. Log off the workgroup server.

Lab 15: Planning the Network

Objectives

After completing this lab, you will be able to

- Examine the networking potential of a building
- Plan a network installation
- Specify the Internet Protocol (IP) addresses and computer names to be used on a new network installation

Note Completing this lab will help reinforce your learning from Chapter 14 of the textbook.

Before You Begin

This lab does not require hands-on use of the computers.

Estimated time to complete the lab: 20 minutes

Exercise 1
Examining a Network Installation Site

In this exercise, you will examine the building where your classroom is located and create a plan for a new network to be installed there.

▶   **To examine a network site**

Imagine that the building your classroom is in has no networking equipment in it and that you are the consultant who has been contracted to design the network that will be installed there. Without intruding into other activities going on in the building, examine the building and its construction, looking at where and how network cables can be installed. Ignore the current network infrastructure and imagine that you are starting completely from scratch.

Once you have examined the building, answer the following questions.

Describe the basic construction of the building (for example, a brick office building, a glass and steel skyscraper, a converted private house, and so on).

_____

_____

_____

How many floors are there in the building?

_____

How many rooms will be networked on each floor? How many rooms are in the entire building?

_____

_____

Describe the internal construction of the building, such as the materials used to build the walls, floors, and ceilings.

_____

_____

_____

How will you run cables to the individual computers in each room?

_____

_____

_____

What hardware will you need for each cable run?

_____

_____

_____

How will you run cables between rooms?

_____

_____

_____

Assuming that the building has multiple floors, how will you run cables between floors?

_____

_____

_____

List any obstructions you find that would affect the installation of the cables (such as fluorescent light fixtures and other electrical equipment).

_____

_____

_____

Exercise 2
Planning the Network

In this exercise, you will use the information you gathered in Exercise 1 to create a plan for the network to be installed in the building.

▶   **To create a network plan**

Your network plan must meet the following requirements:

- Every room in the building will be filled with workers, each of whom will require a computer running Microsoft Windows 2000.
- The network cables must be completely hidden wherever possible.
- The network will consist of separate local area networks (LANs) connected to a backbone network by routers. Each LAN will have no more than 50 workstations connected to it.
- The network must be operational at all times. No part of the network should be rendered unavailable by the failure of a single router.
- The client wants a high-speed network that runs at a minimum of 100 Mbps.
- All of the users on the network must have access to the Internet through a single router connected by an Internet service provider (ISP) using a T-1 leased line.

Basing your design on these requirements, answer the following questions.

How many LANs will you create for the entire project?

_____

How did you decide on the boundaries for each LAN?

_____

_____

_____

What type of cable will you use for the network?

_____

What data-link layer protocol will the network use, and why?

_____

_____

What network layer protocol will the network use, and why?

_____

_____

How will you provide the network fault tolerance that the client requires?

_____

_____

How many routers will you need for the entire project (including the Internet access router)?

_____

Where will each router be located?

_____

_____

_____

How will you run the cables from each room to the router?

_____

_____

_____

What type of cable and what data-link layer protocol will the backbone network use?

_____

_____

Exercise 3
Collecting Information

In this exercise, you will determine the IP addresses and the computer names that the network will use.

▶   **To determine IP addresses and computer names**

For the new network you have planned, you have been assigned the Class B network address 172.28.0.0. Using this address, design a sufficient number of subnets to support your network design, with each LAN and backbone being a separate subnet. Then answer the following questions.

Tip You might want to review the exercises you performed in Lab 9 to answer these questions.

How many subnets do you need for your network design?

_____

What subnet mask will you use for the entire network?

_____

Specify the network address for each of the subnets you will create.

_____

_____

_____

Will the workstations on the subnets require a default gateway address?
Why or why not?

_____

_____

_____

Create a naming system for the computers on the network that identifies the geographical location of the system. Remember that Windows 2000 computer names can be no more than 15 characters long. Then answer the following questions.

How does your naming system identify the floor a computer is on?

_____

_____

How does your naming system identify the room a computer is in?

_____

_____

Lab 16: Installing a Network

Objectives

After completing this lab, you will be able to

- Understand the function of a crossover cable
- Understand the function of a hub's uplink port

Note Completing this lab will help reinforce your learning from Chapter 15 of the textbook.

Before You Begin

This lab assumes that your workgroup is still configured as it was at the end of Lab 14, with the workgroup server and workstation connected to the workgroup hub and the hub connected to the classroom network. Before beginning the exercises in this lab, disconnect the hub from the classroom network by unplugging the cable from the uplink port.

To complete this lab, you will need the following additional hardware:

- One unshielded twisted-pair (UTP) crossover cable

You will also need the following information:

- The password for the Administrator account on your workgroup server and workstation, assigned by your instructor.
- The two-digit number assigned to your workgroup by your instructor. This number is used to form the name of your workgroup (WG*xx*, where *xx* is the number assigned to your workgroup), your workgroup server (WG*xx*Svr), and your workgroup workstation (WG*xx*Wrkstn).

Estimated time to complete the lab: 20 minutes

Exercise 1
Using a Crossover Cable

In this exercise, you will create a two-node network by connecting your workgroup computers together directly, using a crossover cable.

▶   **To create a two-node network**

1. Shut down both of your workgroup computers and make sure the power is off to both machines.

2. Unplug the network cables from the network interface adapters in both computers.

3. Plug one end of the crossover cable into the network interface adapter in the workgroup server and the other end into the network interface adapter in the workgroup workstation.

4. Turn on both computers.

5. When both computers have started, log on to the workgroup workstation as Administrator, using the password supplied by your instructor.

6. On the workgroup workstation, click Start, point to Programs, point to Accessories, and then click Command Prompt.

7. In the Command Prompt window, type **ping WG*xx*Svr** (where *xx* is the number assigned to your workgroup), and then press ENTER.

   What are the results of the ping test?

   _____

   _____

   Why did you receive the results you did?

   _____

   _____

   How did the absence of the hub affect the results of the test?

   _____

   _____

What would happen if you left the original hub configuration in place and simply replaced one of the straight-through cables with a crossover cable?

_____

_____

8. Shut down both computers, and make sure the power is off.

Exercise 2
Using the Uplink Port

In this exercise, you will use your workgroup hub's uplink port to provide the same function as a crossover cable

▶   **To use the uplink port with a crossover cable**

1. Disconnect the crossover cable from your workgroup workstation.

2. Plug one of the straight-through cables still connected to the hub into the network interface adapter of the workgroup workstation.

3. Plug the free end of the crossover cable into one of the hub's standard ports.

   Both computers should now be connected to standard ports in the hub, with the workgroup workstation using a straight-through cable and the server using the crossover cable. This is the same configuration described in the last question in Exercise 1.

4. Turn on both computers.

5. When both computers have started, log on to the workgroup workstation as Administrator, using the password supplied by your instructor.

6. On the workgroup workstation, click Start, point to Programs, point to Accessories, and then click Command Prompt.

7. In the Command Prompt window, type **ping WG*xx*Svr** (where *xx* is the number assigned to your workgroup), and then press ENTER.

   What are the results of the ping test now?

   _____

   _____

   Did you receive the results you predicted in the last question in Exercise 1? Why or why not?

   _____

   _____

Note Some newer hubs have auto-switching uplink ports that automatically implement the crossover circuit as needed. If you are using this type of hub, you will not receive the predicted results in this part of the exercise because the port will adjust itself.

---

8. Unplug the crossover cable from the standard hub port and plug it into the hub's uplink port.

Note If the uplink port on your hub is switched, make sure that the port is configured to function as an uplink port.

How many crossovers are in the circuit between the server and the workstation now?

What do you think the results of the ping test will be now? Why?

9. Perform the ping test again by typing **ping WG***xx***Svr** in the Command Prompt window, and then pressing ENTER.

Were the results of the ping test as you expected?

10. Shut down the workgroup server and make sure the power is off.

11. Unplug the crossover cable from the server's network interface adapter and from the hub.

12. Using your straight-through cable, connect the server to a standard port in the hub.

Lab 17: Performing Network Maintenance Tasks

Objectives

After completing this lab, you will be able to

- Use the Microsoft Windows 2000 Backup program to perform full and incremental backups
- Install a Windows 2000 Service Pack

Note Completing this lab will help reinforce your learning from Chapter 16 of the textbook.

Before You Begin

This lab assumes that your workgroup is still configured as it was at the end of Lab 16, with the workgroup server and workstation connected to the workgroup hub and the hub disconnected from the classroom network.

Before beginning the exercises in this lab, connect the hub to the classroom network by plugging one end of a straight-through cable into the hub's uplink port and the other end into the classroom network jack.

To complete this lab, you will need the following information:

- The password for the Administrator account on your workgroup server, assigned by your instructor

Estimated time to complete the lab: 30 minutes

Exercise 1
Performing a Full Backup

In this exercise, you will use the Windows 2000 Backup program on your workgroup server to back up its hard drive.

▶ **To perform a full backup**

1. Log on to your workgroup server as Administrator, using the password supplied by your instructor.

2. Click Start, point to Programs, point to Accessories, point to System Tools, and then click Backup.

   The Backup dialog box appears.

3. Select the Backup tab.

4. In the left pane of the Backup window, select the check box next to the C: icon.

5. On the Tools menu, select Options.

   The Options dialog box appears.

   What is the backup type chosen by default, and what are its properties?

   _____

   _____

6. Select the Backup Log tab, and then select the Detailed option.

7. Select the Exclude Files tab.

   Note the filespecs that are listed in the Files Excluded For All Users box. Why are these files excluded?

   _____

   _____

8. Click OK to close the Options dialog box.

   What is the value in the Backup Destination drop-down list box?

   _____

   Can you change this setting? Why or why not?

   _____

   _____

9. In the Backup Media Or File Name text box, type **c:\fullbackup.bkf**.

   This backup is being performed for test purposes only. Why should you not perform actual backups in this way?

   _____

   _____

10. Click Start Backup.

    The Backup Job Information dialog box appears.

11. Click Start Backup.

    The backup process begins, and the Backup Progress window appears.

    After several minutes, the backup process is completed and the Backup Progress dialog box appears. What is the status of the backup job?

    _____

12. Click Report.

    The Microsoft Notepad window opens, displaying the backup log.

    How many files have been skipped?

    _____

13. Examine the skipped files listed in the log.

    Tip Use the Find feature in Notepad to locate the log entries containing the word "skipped."

    Why were these files skipped?

    _____

14. On the File menu, select Exit to close the Notepad window.

15. On the Job menu, select Exit to close Windows 2000 Backup.

Exercise 2
Installing a Service Pack

In this exercise, you will install the latest Windows 2000 Service Pack release on your workgroup server.

▶   **To install a Service Pack**

1. Log on to your workgroup server as Administrator, using the password supplied by your instructor.

2. Click Start, point to Programs, point to Accessories, and then click Windows Explorer.

3. On drive C of your workgroup server, create a new subfolder named ServPack beneath the Windist folder.

4. Use Windows Explorer to browse to the Instructor01 server on the classroom network and locate the ServPack share on that computer.

5. Copy the contents of the ServPack folder on Instructor01 to the ServPack folder you just created on your local drive.

6. Double-click the Service Pack distribution file you just copied.

    The Extracting Files progress indicator appears, followed by the Windows 2000 Service Pack Setup dialog box.

7. Select the Accept License Agreement check box.

8. Click Read Me and examine the contents of the file that appears.

9. In the Windows 2000 Service Pack Setup dialog box, click Install.

    A progress indicator window appears. The Service Pack installation process takes several minutes.

10. When a Windows 2000 Service Pack Setup message box appears, click Restart to restart the computer.

Exercise 3
Performing an Incremental Backup

In this exercise, you will perform an incremental backup job on your workgroup server to back up the Service Pack files you just installed.

▶   **To perform an incremental backup**

1. Log on to your workgroup server as Administrator, using the password supplied by your instructor.

2. Click Start, point to Programs, point to Accessories, point to System Tools, and then click Backup.

    The Backup dialog box appears.

3. Select the Backup tab.

4. In the left pane of the Backup window, select the check box next to the C: icon.

5. On the Tools menu, click Options.

    The Options dialog box appears.

6. In the Default Backup Type drop-down menu, select Incremental.

    How does an incremental backup job differ from a full backup?

    _____

    _____

7. Select the Backup Log tab, and then select the Detailed option.

8. Select the Exclude Files tab.

9. In the Files Excluded For All Users box, click Add New.

    The Add Excluded Files dialog box appears.

10. Scroll down the Registered File Type list and select the .bkf extension, and then click OK.

    C:*.bkf is added to the list of excluded files.

    Why was it necessary to do this?

    _____

    _____

11. Click OK to close the Options dialog box.

12. In the Backup Media Or File Name text box, type
    c:\incrementalbackup.bkf.

13. Click Start Backup.

   The Backup Job Information dialog box appears.

14. Click Start Backup.

   The backup process begins, and the Backup Progress window appears.

   After a few moments, the backup process is completed and the Backup Progress dialog box appears. What is the status of the backup job?

   _____

   How many files were backed up?

   _____

   Why are the results different from those in the earlier backup job you performed?

   _____

   _____

15. Click Report.

   The Notepad window opens, displaying the backup log.

16. On the File menu, select Exit to close the Notepad window.

17. On the Job menu, select Exit to close Windows 2000 Backup.

18. Log off the workgroup server.

Lab 18: Implementing Network Troubleshooting Procedures

Objectives

After completing this lab, you will be able to

- Apply an organized troubleshooting process to a real-world problem

Note Completing this lab will help reinforce your learning from Chapter 17 of the textbook.

Before You Begin

This lab assumes that your workgroup is still configured as it was at the end of Lab 17, with the workgroup server and workstation connected to the workgroup hub and the hub connected to the classroom network.

To complete this lab, you will need the following information:

- The password for the Administrator account on your workgroup server and workstation, assigned by your instructor.
- The two-digit number assigned to your workgroup by your instructor. This number is used to form the name of your workgroup (WG*xx*, where *xx* is the number assigned to your workgroup), your workgroup server (WG*xx*Svr), and your workgroup workstation (WG*xx*Wrkstn).

Estimated time to complete the lab: 30 minutes

Exercise 1
Troubleshooting a Networking Problem

In this exercise, you will use your troubleshooting skills to determine what is wrong on your workgroup network, propose a course of action to fix it, and test your results.

► **To troubleshoot a networking problem**

Before you arrived at the lab, your instructor modified something on your workgroup network to make it function improperly, or perhaps not function at all. Your task in this lab is to determine what is wrong and implement a solution, behaving as though you were performing in a professional capacity as part of the network support team. For the purposes of this lab, the troubleshooting process is more important than the solution. Work your way through the troubleshooting process, using the following general steps:

1. Establish the symptoms.

2. Identify the affected area.

3. Establish what has changed.

4. Select the most probable cause.

5. Implement a solution.

6. Test the result.

7. Recognize the potential effects of the solution.

8. Document the solution.

As you proceed through the process, be sure to document your actions at every step and be logical in your progression through the possible causes of the problem you are experiencing.

Use the following procedure to perform the troubleshooting process.

1. Log on to your workgroup server as Administrator, using the password supplied by your instructor.

2. Using one of the techniques you employed in the previous labs, such as the ping test, check the server's connectivity to the workgroup workstation.

   What are the results of the connectivity test?

   _____

   _____

What error messages did you receive when testing the connectivity?

_____

_____

_____

3. To identify the area affected by the problem, check the server's connectivity to the classroom network. What is the result?

_____

_____

_____

4. Log on to your workgroup workstation as Administrator, using the password supplied by your instructor.

5. Test the workstation's connectivity with the workgroup server and with the classroom network. What are the results?

_____

_____

_____

What conclusions can you draw from these additional connectivity test results?

_____

_____

_____

6. Starting with the most likely location of the problem, begin checking the hardware and software components involved in network communications to determine what has changed since the network was last operational.

In the space below, list each of the elements you checked, in the order you checked them; specify how you checked them; and then indicate whether each element is correctly configured or is a possible cause of the problem.

_____

_____

_____

_____

_____

_____

_____

_____

_____

7. Once you have completely checked the networking components, select the most likely cause of the problem and, in the space below, write down what you think you must do to resolve the problem.

_____

_____

_____

8. Make the changes you have proposed and test your solution by performing the same diagnostic tests you used earlier in this exercise. What were the results?

_____

_____

_____

9. If your solution was unsuccessful, document your results and return to step 6 to try to find the correct solution (using the next most likely location of the problem).

10. Once you have located the source of the problem and corrected it, document the entire case in the space below, including the source of the problem, the possible cause, and the steps you took to resolve it.

_____

_____

_____

_____

_____

_____

_____

_____

_____

_____

_____

_____

11. Log off the workgroup server and the workgroup workstation.

Lab 19: Using Network Troubleshooting Tools

Objectives

After completing this lab, you will be able to

- Monitor network activity using the Microsoft Windows 2000 Performance console

Note Completing this lab will help reinforce your learning from Chapter 18 of the textbook.

Before You Begin

This lab assumes that your workgroup is still configured as it was at the end of Lab 18, with the workgroup server and workstation connected to the workgroup hub and the hub connected to the classroom network.

To complete this lab, you will need the following information:

- The password for the Administrator account on your workgroup server and workstation, assigned by your instructor.
- The two-digit number assigned to your workgroup by your instructor. This number is used to form the name of your workgroup (WG*xx*, where *xx* is the number assigned to your workgroup), your workgroup server (WG*xx*Svr), and your workgroup workstation (WG*xx*Wrkstn).

Estimated time to complete the lab: 30 minutes

Exercise 1
Using System Monitor

In this exercise, you will use the System Monitor tool in the Performance console to display information about the computer's network activity.

▶ **To use System Monitor**

1. Log on to your workgroup server as Administrator, using the password supplied by your instructor.

2. Click Start, point to Programs, point to Administrative Tools, and then click Performance.

   The Performance console appears.

3. With the System Monitor icon selected in the left pane, click the + (add) button in the right pane's toolbar.

   The Add Counters dialog box appears.

4. In the Performance Object drop-down list, select Network Interface.

5. In the Select Instances From List box, click the entry representing your network interface adapter (not the MS TCP Loopback Interface entry).

6. Under Select Counters From List, select Bytes Received/Sec, and then click Add; then select Bytes Sent/Sec, and then click Add.

7. Click Close.

   What do you see in the main System Monitor display?

   _____

   _____

8. Log on to your workgroup workstation as Administrator, using the password supplied by your instructor.

9. On the workgroup workstation, click Start, point to Programs, point to Accessories, and then click Windows Explorer.

10. Copy the \Windist folder on the workstation's drive C to drive C on the workgroup server, overwriting the existing files as needed.

    What do you see in the System Monitor display on the workgroup server now?

    _____

    _____

Which of the two counters you added shows greater activity? Why?

_____

_____

How do you explain the relatively constant levels of the Bytes Sent/Sec counter, as compared with the widely fluctuating levels of the Bytes Received/Sec counter?

_____

_____

Exercise 2
Comparing TCP and ICMP Traffic Levels

In this exercise, you will monitor the levels of Transmission Control Protocol (TCP) and Internet Control Message Protocol (ICMP) traffic on the workgroup server and modify the System Monitor display to view that traffic.

▶   **To view TCP and ICMP traffic levels**

1. On the workgroup server, select the Bytes Received/Sec counter at the bottom of the System Monitor display, and then click the X (delete) button in the right pane's toolbar to remove the counter. Do the same for the Bytes Sent/Sec counter.

2. Click the + (add) button in the toolbar.

   The Add Counters dialog box appears.

3. In the Performance Object drop-down list, select TCP.

4. Under Select Counters From List, select Segments/Sec, and then click Add.

5. In the Performance Object drop-down list, select ICMP.

6. Under Select Counters From List, select Messages/Sec, and then click Add.

7. Click Close.

8. On the workgroup workstation, repeat the file copy procedure you performed in Exercise 1.

   On the workgroup server, what activity do you see in the System Monitor display?

   _____

   _____

9. Right-click anywhere on the System Monitor graph, and then select Properties.

   The System Monitor Properties dialog box appears.

10. Select the Graph tab; then in the Vertical Scale box, increase the value in the Maximum text box to 200, and then click OK.

    What happens to the graph? Why?

    _____

    _____

11. On the workgroup workstation, click Start, point to Programs, point to Accessories, and then click Command Prompt.

12. In the Command Prompt window, type **ping WGxxSvr -n 1000** (where *xx* is the number assigned to your workgroup), and then press ENTER.

    On the workgroup server, what activity do you see for the ICMP Messages/Sec counter on the graph?

    _____

13. Click the ICMP Messages/Sec counter in the list at the bottom of the display.

    What value appears in the Average box right above the counter list?

    _____

    Why do you not see this activity on the graph?

    _____

14. Open the System Monitor Properties dialog box again; in the Graph tab, change the Maximum Vertical Scale value to 5, and then click OK.

    What happens to the graph now?

    _____

15. Log off the workgroup server and the workgroup workstation.